The book of the year
about the mystery man
of the century!

HOWARD HUGHES: THE HIDDEN YEARS

In a startling eyewitness account by two of the aides who were closest to Hughes in those long years of secrecy comes a story even more grotesque than the wildest rumors about him. Here is the first authentic account of why Hughes suddenly fled his penthouse hideout in Las Vegas and fired his $520,000-a-year chief executive, Robert Maheu. The aide who engineered it recounts Hughes's wild hairbreadth escape from the Britannia Beach Hotel in Nassau. And, beyond the insider's view of the man's peculiar eating and grooming habits, his "insulation" against germs, the drugs he injected into himself, the book offers an extraordinary insight into the pivotal role he played in American life by "one of the best investigative reporters of his generation," James Phelan.

An "enterprising work of reportage . . . appalling . . . tantalizing . . . fascinating."
—*The New York Times*

HOWARD HUGHES: THE HIDDEN YEARS

James Phelan

WARNER BOOKS

A Warner Communications Company

FOR
Amalie, Judy
AND
Janet

I met a traveller from an antique land
Who said: Two vast and trunkless legs of stone
Stand in the desert. Near them on the sand
Half sunk, a shatter'd visage lies . . .
And on the pedestal these words appear:
'My name is Ozymandias, king of kings:
Look on my words, ye Mighty, and despair!'
Nothing beside remains. Round the decay
Of that colossal wreck, boundless and bare,
The lone and level sands stretch far away.

—From *Ozymandias,* by P. B. Shelley

FOREWORD

Howard Hughes's greatest invention was not the world's largest flying boat, or flush-riveting for planes, or Jane Russell's cantilevered bra. It was his Secrecy Machine. Unlike his great flying boat, which barely got off the water, his Secrecy Machine functioned almost flawlessly for fifteen years. It made of Hughes, one of the best-known men in the world, a man about whose later life almost nothing was truly known.

Only a very rich man could afford such a Secrecy Machine, and only Howard Hughes wanted and needed one. This book is about how it worked, some of the things it hid, and why he needed it.

It had many parts, because he had many secrets to hide. He hid women, business transactions, old planes and cars, his thoughts, his whereabouts, what he looked like, the uses to which he put his money, praiseworthy or disreputable. He hid big secrets, such as a $100,000 cash bribe for a President, and trivial ones, such as where he obtained his apple strudel. He hid a California detective in Australia for years, paying him $1,000 a month just to conceal what the detective had done for him.

He hid his own motives, so that even those closest to him did not know why he was doing what he did. In an age that exploded into personal openness, self-revelation, letting it all hang out, he believed in tucking it all away.

Mainly he hid himself. He did this so well that a con man, Clifford Irving, was able to fabricate his own Hughes out of newspaper clippings, scraps of other people's memories, and great swatches of pure fiction, and then sell an autobiography of this fake Hughes to a publisher for $750,000. That Irving's fraudulent Hughes was pronounced genuine by both McGraw-Hill and the editors of Time-Life attests to the dearth of knowledge of the real Hughes.

An earlier generation mistook him for a blend of Charles Lindbergh, Tom Swift and his Electric Locomotive, and Jimmy Stewart in *Mr. Smith Goes to Washington,* and made him an American folk hero. When he faced down a hostile congressional investigating committee after World War II, a brief Hughes-for-President movement sprang up—while he was secretly corrupting political and governmental processes.

Today's feverish cult of the conspiracy pictures him as an American folk demon. They see him as a giant puppet master, a one-man Illuminati manipulating this nation and others. If he was not the master of the CIA, they cry, he was at least its premier agent. Norman Mailer, in a febrile essay entitled "A Harlot High and Low," could not decide which Hughes was, but never entertained the possibility that he was neither. "He could not know," Mailer wrote, "and no one looking on from the outside could know, how much of the CIA was part of his operation or how much of his operation was directed by the CIA. Indeed, was there even a live man named Hughes at the center of it all, or was there a Special Committee?"

Mailer speculated that there was no live Hughes. Others *knew* that Howard Hughes died long ago. Over the years hundreds of people expressed this conviction to me. A group in Texas claimed to have, but never produced, a copy of his death certificate, issued in 1959 and signed by a medical doctor. Others offered contemporary photographs of the Hughes the Texans said was long dead. Logic compelled the conclusion that either the death certificate or the photographs were fake. Time proved them all vaporous. "Hughes was the only man I ever knew who had to die to prove he had been alive," said Walter Kane, a long-time Hughes employee.

Much of this vapor was an unintended by-product of the Hughes Secrecy Machine. The vacuum of fact filled with fiction. Secrecy generated myths, and the myths then bred incestuously. The unseen and unknown fascinates and frightens. What people thought they glimpsed at Loch Ness, and no one could find, must have been a monster. Strange things that flashed across the sky but never landed became flying saucers, then space ships from other galaxies, then chariots of the gods.

Howard Hughes was a real man, one of the strangest of his times. He was born December 24, 1905, vanished from public view in his middle fifties, and died April 5, 1976, on a plane bound for a hospital in Houston, Texas. His career, before he disappeared into his Secrecy Machine, is so well known that it needs no more than the briefest summary. He inherited a highly profitable oil-well drilling bit enterprise, Hughes Tool Co., from his father when he was a young man. Early in his career he made movies —*Hell's Angels, Scarface,* and *The Outlaw* were the best known. He was a superb flier and plane buff who set many records, built the world's largest flying boat, and put together an international airline, TWA.

He intrigued many, infuriated others, and became densely encrusted with legends, because he was one of the richest men on our planet, was enormously willful, scorned society and its customs and laws, marched to his own offbeat drum, and stubbornly remained invisible. From his hidden aerie, he acquired enormous wealth, seemingly by magic, while others rode subways and freeways and grubbed a livelihood. He always seemed larger than life because he could gratify any whim. He had an insatiable lust for power that begat many whims, some childlike and absurd, some Machiavellian and malevolent. What most set him apart from the masses was that the whims he chose to gratify were not those that the masses fantasized for themselves.

Foreword

Joan Didion, who onces lived near his Romaine Street headquarters in Hollywood, the former control center for his Secrecy Machine, wrote of Hughes in her *Slouching Towards Bethlehem:*

> It is impossible to think of Howard Hughes without seeing the apparently bottomless gulf between what we say we want and what we do want, between what we officially admire and secretly desire . . . In a nation which increasingly appears to prize social virtues, Howard Hughes remains not merely antisocial but grandly, brilliantly, surpassingly asocial. He is the last private man, the dream we no longer admit.

But he was not truly a private man, as was the gold prospector who hit it rich, built a castle in the fastnesses of a remote desert valley, and put a wall around it posted "Stay Away!"

The concept of Hughes as a free-enterprising maverick, an entrepreneurial loner who built a great fortune by rugged individualism and a gambler's daring, is pure myth. It is a myth that he cultivated and exploited. But in a number of court tests Hughes was declared to be a public figure in that he had injected himself into the public arena by his own actions. His affairs were intricately entwined with those of government on federal, state and local levels, and it was Hughes who so entwined them. He did so for the same reason Willie Sutton robbed banks—because that was where the money was.

For thirty years he siphoned huge sums out of the public treasury. Since 1965, according to a 1975 study of government records by Donald Barlett and

James Steele of Knight News Service, Hughes's companies had received more than $6 billion in contracts from the federal government—an average siphoning of $1.7 million every day. He was long the beneficiary of favors, licenses, franchises, and subsidies underwritten by taxpayers' money. He facilitated his access to public funds by private cash payments to politicians and government officials.

What he wanted and accomplished was to enrich himself from public funds and government favors while scorning the public and defying the government that had enriched him. He did this through his Secrecy Machine, and by living from 1970 outside the boundaries of the United States, beyond the reach of the law.

This nation deposed, in a single administration, a Vice-President and a President. But in a quarter-century it was not able to force Hughes to show up in court, give a sworn deposition, or appear before any governmental agency. No one could subpoena or arrest an invisible man.

Journalists faced a similar problem. How could one report on a man no one could see? They were impelled to try because many of his secrets affected the citizenry and their government and hence belonged in the public domain.

Hughes wanted nothing written about him that he could not control. To gratify his wish, Hughes's chief counsel, Chester Davis, invented in 1966 a contrivance called Rosemont Enterprises, Inc.

Davis maintained that Rosemont owned "sole and exclusive right to use or publish [Hughes's] name, likeness, personality, life story, or incidents therein."

"The publication of any story about Mr. Hughes," he went on, "would appear to invade such rights, even if the matters therein are assumed to be factually accurate." This was the ultimate act of secrecy and acquisition, to own and keep from others the facts of his life.

One night at dinner in Greenwich Village Davis explained this to me as "the Joe DiMaggio bat theory."

"If you are going to put out a bat with Joe Di-Maggio's name on it," Davis declared, "you have to get DiMaggio's permission and pay DiMaggio a royalty."

Because books, unlike baseball bats, are protected by the First Amendment to the U.S. Constitution, Davis's contention has been rejected by every court in which Rosemont has pressed its claim. Yet Davis's firm still writes what the publishing industry has come to term the "Don't You Dare" letter. Although legally absurd, this book-aborting device is not wholly ineffective. The mere prospect of having to go to court against the well-financed Hughes attorneys discourages marginal publishers reluctant or unable to finance a court fight even though they are certain of winning it.

The core, the *sine qua non* of the Secrecy Machine in Hughes's final years was his cadre of senior aides, the "Mormon Mafia" or "Palace Guard." They were the men who were believed to be the only humans who ever saw or talked in person to the billionaire. They moved him about unglimpsed, controlled access by telephone or letter to him, and manned the inner ramparts surrounding his hiding place.

At what proved to be a major crisis and pivotal point in Hughes's life, his flight from Las Vegas, this elite group acquired some supporting functionaries who also saw and talked to Hughes. They were brought in because the task of keeping Hughes hidden became simultaneously more difficult and more imperative. The primary function of the Palace Guard was to allay the severest of Hughes's many fears, quirks, eccentricities, madnesses. That was his *scopophobia,* or fear of being looked at.

The Machine malfunctioned during the 1970 crisis, was repaired, and then broke down after his death. On both occasions, I became the recipient of the spillage because of my long interest in Hughes.

For twenty years I wrote about Hughes for many magazines, covered his activities for newspapers, including *The New York Times,* and compiled a five-foot-thick file on Hughes, his associates, his enterprises. When I first started writing about Hughes one of his agents tried to buy me off with an open-end check and an offer of free and unlimited flights on Hughes's TWA. I rejected the only bribe tendered to me in a lifetime as a reporter. Thereafter the Secrecy Machine contented itself with balefully monitoring me; twice the Hughes agents obtained copies of my manuscripts before they reached my publishers.

Three weeks after the death of Hughes I received a late-night telephone call. The call culminated, after certain ritualistic maneuvers that anything involving Hughes seems to inspire, in a meeting with two men.

They were Gordon Margulis and Mell Stewart, who have contributed significantly to the material for this book. Margulis had ten years in Hughes's service, Stewart fifteen. At the beginning they were at the perimeter of the Hughes inner circle, but in his last and most carefully hidden years they were inside it. They saw Hughes, talked to him, ministered to him personally. At the end it was Margulis who lifted the dying billionaire's wasted body onto the plane for his final flight.

Because of the Clifford Irving hoax, the forgeries, fake photographs, and assorted trompes l'oeil that abound in the world of Hughes, I subjected the two men to a series of verbal litmus tests, which they endured with admirable patience.

They had certain documents with them. They produced passports showing their entries and exits from the many countries where Hughes had been taken in his final years. They knew people outsiders could not have known, incidents that had never been reported, dates that could not be guessed at. Frequently they knew what had happened inside the Hughes enclave —events that I had observed firsthand from the outside—and the two halves fitted together exactly. The ultimate authentication of Margulis and Stewart came when Summa Corporation officials learned they were talking to a writer. They were summoned to Summa headquarters and were later requested to meet with the full Summa board of directors. Both refused.

This book embodies their experiences within the Hughes sanctum. For the first time, they open the door the Secrecy Machine kept locked, chained, and guarded.

17

They saw Hughes as only a handful of men ever saw him, and they came to pity him and wanted to tell why. Others who saw him have bonds of loyalty to Summa Corporation and contractual restrictions that do not bind Stewart and Margulis.

Isolated with Hughes, they had limited knowledge of the Hughes organization beyond his sealed-off quarters. In many instances, astonishingly, so did Howard Hughes. What they had, however, was of singular value: familiarity with the man rather than The Man, the person instead of The Legend.

The thrust of this book, its context, and some hitherto unpublished material come from the author. Part of the material is from sources that cannot be acknowledged, a practice I, as a journalist, generally oppose, but they can be neither acknowledged nor thanked without risking reprisals against them. They know who they are, and have my gratitude.

I am grateful primarily to Gordon Margulis and Mell Stewart, and also to Wallace Turner, San Francisco bureau chief of *The New York Times* and its Hughes expert. For years we tracked Hughes, sometimes in competition and sometimes together. My respect for him and thanks for his help are unstinted.

He knew, better than most reporters, how much was hidden and unknown in the life of Hughes and how much it needed to be known in a nation that proclaims itself to be open and self-governing. Hughes exemplified and helped to shape an era of deception and manipulation that convulsed this country.

"Someday it will all come pouring out," Turner

often said, affirming the credo that sustains a dedicated reporter.

This book is the beginning.

—JAMES PHELAN

CONTENTS

HOWARD HUGHES: THE HIDDEN YEARS

[1]
DEATH
OF A BILLIONAIRE

The naked, motionless body on the bed was that of Howard Robard Hughes, one of the richest men in the world. On Saturday, April 3, 1976, he was less than forty-eight hours from his death, and he was dying the way he had lived, secretly and in incredible isolation.

None of the conventional human gestures or rituals for the dying attended his last hours. There were no flowers or get-well cards or phone calls from solicitous friends. He had no friends because he had never sought or valued friends. And no one except a tight little group of silent men knew that he was even ill.

He lay hidden away in the latest and the last of the blacked-out rooms that had been his home for many years. The bedroom, in the twentieth-floor penthouse suite at the Acapulco Princess Hotel, was cloned from all the blacked-out rooms that had preceded it.

Thick draperies, their borders sealed to the walls with masking tape, shut out the world. The Acapulco Princess is a luxury hotel in Mexico's internationally known beach resort and a favorite playground of the rich. But none of the carefree sights or sounds from the beach or the landscaped tropical gardens below penetrated to the sealed bedroom. It was dark, silent, timeless, a room that could have been anywhere or nowhere, a setting out of Kafka.

Facing Hughes at the foot of his bed, as always, was his movie screen. Behind his bed, as always, was his movie projector. Alongside the bed was his special amplifier for the movie sound track, its controls in easy reach. For years he had lain in bed watching movies, immersed in a series of two-dimensional worlds that he chose himself and totally controlled. He ran his favorites over and over, the sound turned up to accommodate his impaired hearing, the dialogue booming and reverberating in the darkened room. He had run his No. 1 choice, *Ice Station Zebra*, more than 150 times, until his functionaries knew the entire sound track by heart. But now the screen was dark, the amplifier silent.

Near his bed were stacks of what he called "insulation," endlessly replenished boxes of Kleenex and paper kitchen towels he used to shield himself from the real, unruly, unclean world.

He had hidden himself away in his blacked-out rooms for more than fifteen years, generating a vast body of folklore, myths, and fabrications about why he had become the world's best-known invisible man.

He was a figure of Gothic horror, a nightmare of self-neglect, emaciated from his bizarre eating habits, unkempt, unbarbered, ravaged by drugs. Ten years earlier, in the words of a man who had seen him then for the first time, he had looked "like a witch's brother." In recent months he had deteriorated even further. His body was starved, dehydrated, and atrophied to a pitiful skeleton resembling those of the victims of Dachau and Buchenwald. He weighed barely ninety pounds. His one-time 6' 4" frame had shrunk three inches. His legs and arms were pipestem thin, so fragile that a strong child might have snapped them like a wishbone. On his back were two severe bedsores that had plagued him for years. His pelvis jutted sharply, uncushioned by flesh. On his right side one could see the outline of a metal surgical pin that had repaired, after a fashion, the hip bone he had snapped more than two years earlier in a fall. Since then he had not walked a step, or attempted the exercises prescribed by the operating surgeon. As a consequence, his right knee joint had congealed and would barely bend.

His blood pressure was down disastrously, so low that the next day a doctor would not be able to locate the pulse in his shrunken wrist. His parchment-like skin had the cold, bloodless, waxen look of death.

Into the room came one of his personal aides, Gordon Margulis. He was a ruggedly fit Englishman in his early forties, broad-shouldered with a tapered waist, quiet, self-confident. He had served Howard Hughes for ten years and since the hip fracture had carried Hughes about whenever he had to leave his bed.

Margulis knew that intruding unsummoned into

the blacked-out bedroom violated the rules that prevailed in Hughes's constricted and controlled little world. But for seven weeks, since Hughes and his tight little entourage had unexpectedly quit the Bahamas and flown down to Acapulco, Margulis had sensed that there was something wrong, something dreadfully out of joint. Hughes was now plainly plummeting toward death, and no one was confronting the crisis and coping with it. As Margulis explained it later, "I said to myself, screw the bloody rules."

Margulis stood inside the bedroom door, a dozen feet or so from his employer. He could see the shallow rise and fall of Hughes's thin chest. He watched the figure on the bed for four or five minutes. Then Hughes opened his eyes and stared for a long time at the ceiling. Finally he turned his head to the left, away from Margulis. He reached out a thin arm to a Kleenex box and took out a hypodermic syringe tucked in under the open flap. It was filled with a clear liquid. Hughes held it for a while in his left hand, contemplating it. He turned it several times and tilted it, as if to assure himself that the syringe was charged. Then he reached across his chest and inserted the needle laterally into the outside of his right arm alongside the shrunken bicep.

The movement apparently exhausted him. He fumbled clumsily with the plunger but couldn't depress it. He tried several times and gave up. The syringe hung for a moment from his right arm, and then dropped to the bed.

Margulis turned and went back into the adjoining room. The room was known as The Office.

Like the blacked-out bedroom, it conformed to a long-established pattern. The Office was headquarters for the inner circle of six senior personal aides to Hughes. The Office always immediately adjoined the Hughes bedroom and was always sealed off from the rest of whatever series of suites and rooms housed the entourage. This pattern had been set ten years earlier in Las Vegas, when Hughes had been spirited unseen up to the ninth-floor penthouse of the Desert Inn for a four-year stay. In all the moves thereafter, from Las Vegas to Nassau, from Nassau to Nicaragua, up to Vancouver, back to Nicaragua, over to London, down to the Bahamas, and finally out to Acapulco, the arrangement was always the same. There was the sealed-off headquarters on the top floor of a hotel. At the elevator door was an armed guard, stationed before a locked door barring access to the rest of the floor. Whenever the hotel layout did not accommodate this arrangement, a special partition was built to seal off the rest of the suite from the elevator landing. The guard himself was not allowed in the inner sanctum. From his desk the guard passed on into the suite only the members of the entourage. He also monitored the roof and the fire exits by remote closed-circuit television. Inside the suite was the locked Office of the senior aides, and beyond The Office, the blacked-out bedroom of Howard Hughes.

When the existence of the senior aides had first leaked to the outside world, the press had labeled this elite group the "Palace Guard" and the "Mormon Mafia." "They are men without mouths," said a reporter who once dined with four of them. "They give the impression that if you were to ask whether Hughes had one head and two arms, they would refuse to tell you."

There was always at least one senior aide on duty, twenty-four hours a day, seven days a week. On this day the aide on duty was George Francom. Francom was Gordon Margulis's favorite among the senior aides.

"He's awake, George," Gordon told him. "He's trying to inject himself with his syringe."

The two went into Hughes's bedroom. Hughes, almost deaf without a hearing aid, didn't hear the two men come in. Francom moved alongside the bed. Hughes turned his head and stared at him.

"I didn't get it," he said, making a weak gesture toward his right arm. He was not aware that the syringe had fallen from his arm. "Give it to me, George," he said.

Francom shook his head firmly. "That's a doctor's job," he said. Although Hughes couldn't hear him, he could see his gesture of refusal. He turned to Margulis. "Give me all of it, Gordon," he commanded.

"I won't fool with that crap," Gordon told Francom, and turned to walk out.

"Hey, Gordon," Hughes called weakly. "Hey, ay, ay, ay."

Margulis left the room. Shortly Francom joined him in The Office, shaking his head in distress. He went to a phone and talked earnestly into it. After a while one of the three doctors on stand-by rapped on the door of The Office and was admitted. He went into Hughes's bedroom and was there a long while.

Gordon didn't join him. He had known about the

drug injections for years. One of his jobs was to try to get Hughes to eat with some semblance of normalcy, and one day he had come upon Hughes and his syringe by happenstance. At first Hughes had hidden the syringe away whenever he saw Gordon. But after a while he abandoned his dissembling and had shot himself up openly in Gordon's presence. He gave himself the injections without a doctor in attendance, which Gordon knew was not proper medical practice. Hughes used the syringe in his arm and also, in a routine that made Gordon cringe, shot drugs into his groin, usually on the upper inside of his thighs.

He had a special Kleenex box where he kept the syringe tucked out of sight, and a large metal box that he called "my medication." Margulis did not know what the syringe contained, or what drugs, medicine, or pills were kept in the metal box. His best friend in the Hughes entourage, Mell Stewart, served as a sort of male nurse for Hughes, but Stewart knew little more about the contents of the metal box than Margulis. Stewart said that Hughes consumed awesome quantities of Empirin, a common non-prescription painkiller, and Empirin-codeine. The latter was a prescribed drug, because codeine is an opium derivative and an addictive narcotic. In recent years, Stewart told Margulis, Hughes had begun to use, or had been put on, the new drug Valium. Stewart said that giving Hughes Valium puzzled him.

Valium was developed to combat tension, but it is also a powerful soporific for some people. It swiftly reduces tension and muffles alertness. It is rated a dangerous drug and is sold only on a doctor's prescription. Normally, it is given in tiny five-milligram tablets, or even half tablets, because some people react sensitively to small amounts. There were times when Hughes slept, or lapsed into a drugged coma, for twenty-four or forty-eight hours at a time.

He also recently had periods, both Margulis and Stewart had observed, of what appeared to be a sort of manic "high." He was then at the opposite end from the relaxed, comatose state induced by Valium. He would be awake and restless, would hum constantly and talk disjointedly to himself. Earlier that day he had rambled on and on about some insurance policies. Francom had told Margulis, "Maybe this is something important," and had asked him to go and get a tape recorder. But when he had returned with the recorder, Hughes had lapsed back down into silence.

Hughes's drugs were the province of the doctors, or at least some of the doctors. There were four in the Hughes entourage, but they were not on an equal footing or in agreement about their patient. There had been an argument with one of them because he had refused to apply for a narcotics license, and this had angered Hughes.

"Fire the son of a bitch," Hughes had ordered. Then he added, as he usually did when someone had achieved close access to him, "but keep him on the payroll." By retaining people he had "fired" on his payroll, he kept a rein on them, so they would not go off and disclose any of his secrets to the outside world. His past was strewn with an awesome array of such remittance men (and women). So the "fired" doctor had stayed on with the entourage and a new doctor, who had a narcotics license, was brought in. Gordon wasn't even certain that the recalcitrant doctor had been told that he had been "fired." Firing a man and continuing to pay him was a meaningless gesture except to Hughes, who seemed to regard it as a double exercise of his will and power.

Others of the Palace Guard were also involved somehow with Hughes's drugs and metal "medication" box, Margulis and Stewart had observed. From time to time, certain aides would bring in sealed packets or envelopes to replenish or add to whatever was in the metal box. These packets were referred to cryptically as "The Man's goodies."

They did these things, and performed other peculiar tasks, without explaining to the rest of the entourage what they were doing. The private world of Hughes was rigidly hierarchical, and as compartmentalized as the CIA. Orders would originate somewhere, either with Hughes or with his far-off and seldom-seen "prime minister," Frank William (Bill) Gay. The orders would be passed down the line and carried out without cross-communication among the compartments of functionaries. Those who received or executed the orders down the line usually did not know who had originated them.

Gay was the third "prime minister" or administrative right-hand man for Howard Hughes in a half-century. The first was Noah Dietrich, a stocky, white-thatched financial genius and self-proclaimed "hatchet man" who had served Hughes for thirty-two years. He and Hughes had a bitter parting of the ways in 1957. After Dietrich's departure, Gay had risen steadily in power toward the vacated prime-ministership. Hughes had then unexpectedly and suddenly awarded the premiership to Robert Aime Maheu. Bob Maheu was a genial, well-connected professional "problem solver" with convenient connections at high levels in Washington, including a covert relationship with the CIA. Maheu had been deposed in December, 1970, by a Byzantine power play in which Gay had played a major role. Gay then had moved swiftly into the prime-minister vacancy he had helped create.

When Hughes lay dying in Acapulco, Gay had held the reins in the Hughes empire for more than five years. He was a power in the Mormon Church and had staffed the top echelons of the Hughes empire, especially the elite Palace Guard, with fellow Mormons. Gay was a retiring, reticent man who shunned newsmen and made few public appearances. He had risen to the top of the empire from near the very bottom; he had started as a lowly driver for Hughes's personal secretary, Nadine Henley, back in the 1940's.

Gay was now executive vice-president of Summa Corporation, the parent company that owned and operated almost all of the billionaire's vast holdings. Gay was the senior officer in the three-member executive committee that ran Summa. The second member of this potent triumvirate was Nadine Henley, who had also had a long, steady, and rewarding rise in the Hughes empire. Insiders had observed and envied the way Gay and Mrs. Henley had climbed the empire ladder together and with effective mutual assistance. "Nadine sees Bill Gay as the son she never had," said one Summa insider, "and she made him what he is."

The fact that they had started from the lowest echelons did not mean that they were without considerable talent. "Don't let Bill Gay's mousy air delude you," said one fallen-by-the-wayside Hughesman. "He's a genius at corporate politics and survivorship. And Nadine has the charm of a Richelieu, the mind of a computer, and the memory of an elephant."

Third man in the Summa triumvirate was Chester Davis, head of the New York law firm of Davis and Cox and chief counsel for Summa. Davis was a brilliant, abrasive trial lawyer with a quick mind and a sandpaper tongue. He derived his power in the Hughes empire from his successful handling of the marathon litigation between Hughes and the Eastern financial community over Trans World Airlines. He had lost the case all the way up the judicial ladder to the U.S. Supreme Court. Then, in a stunning reversal, the Supreme Court had nullified a default judgment against Hughes that totaled, with penalties and interest, more than $160 million. Davis's position in the empire, accordingly, was much like that of a baseball player who had poled out the World Series-winning home run in the bottom of the ninth inning in the final game. Thereafter he was untouchable.

Hughes was sole stockholder in Summa. But the triumvirate ran it from a little-known and unpublicized headquarters in an office building in Encino, California, a suburb of Los Angeles. Their decisions were ostensibly subject to the approval of Summa's board of directors, but the Davis-Gay-Henley troika themselves constituted a majority of the five-member board. The other two board members were two senior aides from the Palace Guard, John Holmes and Levar Myler. Both of them, like the other senior aides, owed their positions to Bill Gay.

This simple corporate structure—given Hughes's sole ownership of Summa—gave unchallengeable power, unparalleled in any other major American corporation, to the Encino triumvirate. With no public holdings whatever in Summa, only the solitary stockholder, Hughes, was entitled to any accounting. And the lone stockholder was sealed away from the world and dependent for information on a Palace Guard loyal to and controlled by Bill Gay and Mrs. Henley.

The line of communication between Encino and the isolated billionaire ran through a man named Kay Glenn. Glenn was unmarried, a bachelor in his forties, a man given to striking graceful poses. He held the purse strings of the Hughes entourage and served as Gay's plenipotentiary and overseer of the Palace Guard. Glenn was stationed at Encino with Bill Gay, but shuttled back and forth between Encino and the wandering entourage when the need arose or some crisis developed.

The six senior aides in the Palace Guard, collectively, ran the entourage. They had immediate access to Hughes, from their Office adjoining his bedroom, and controlled the flow of information as simply as if they had their hands on a faucet. Through a constantly manned telephone room always close by The Office, they had direct and exclusive communication with Gay and Nadine Henley in Encino. After leaving Las Vegas in 1970, Hughes largely abandoned personal use of the telephone.

The Palace Guard consisted of John Holmes, the senior aide, and under him Howard Eckersley, George Francom, Levar Myler, Clarence "Chuck" Waldron, and James Rickard. Like Bill Gay and Kay Glenn, all were Mormons except Holmes, who was a Catholic.

A tight little group operationally, the Palace Guard was a mixed group of personalities.

Holmes was a loner, highly conservative, close-fisted with money, a tense chain-smoker when out of Hughes's presence. Smoking was just one of a long list of Hughes taboos; others included eating pork or touching him without the use of intervening "insulation."

Eckersley was a genial, good-looking extrovert who got along well with his colleagues. He had a large family, with brigades of sons, daughters, nephews, nieces, and in-laws he was constantly seeking jobs for on a Hughes payroll. He had a penchant for outside business deals and had declined in favor in the Hughes empire when a mining venture he headed erupted into a major scandal on the Canadian Stock Exchange.

Levar Myler was a dour, paunchy, bespectacled man afflicted occasionally with gout. He kept to himself most of the time off duty, a trait that his colleagues respected and approved. He had a single known vice: he was an awesome consumer of Coca-Cola.

Francom was everyone's favorite, friendly, non-aggressive, a devout Mormon who devoted his spare time to reading books on religion, snorkeling in the tropical waters of the Bahamas and Acapulco, and going on nature walks.

Waldron was the latest addition to the Palace Guard. He was a close friend of the entourage's bachelor overseer, Kay Glenn, and a fastidious dresser who devoted hours to his personal grooming. Unlike the other Hughesmen, who maintained a low profile in public, Waldron was an attention-seeker who tried to impress outsiders by flashing large sums of money. He also was given to spurts of behavior that embarrassed his colleagues. Sometimes he would burst into falsetto song, dance alone to music in public places, or suddenly begin to imitate a horse neighing or a dog barking.

The sixth senior aide was Jim Rickard. He had formerly worked on a logging crew in Montana and had operated a small-town movie house. He had started out in the Hughes organization as a Chevrolet driver at the old Hughes headquarters at 7000 Romaine Street in Hollywood.

Romaine, as it was known throughout the Hughes empire, had been the billionaire's legendary "message center" back in the 1950's and 60's. It had served as a sort of St. Cyr Academy or West Point that turned out future officers in the Hughes service. After advancing from chauffeur for Nadine Henley, Bill Gay had been in charge of the drivers and couriers at Romaine back in the days when it was the busy nerve center of the Hughes empire. Among Hughes defectors and cast-asides Gay was called "King of the Chevy Drivers," and his loyal, taciturn Palace Guard appointees were referred to as "Gay's Nebbishes."

Like Bill Gay and Nadine Henley, none of the Palace Guard had any notable previous business or executive experience. Holmes, for example, had been a potato-chip salesman, and Myler had been an Air Force mechanic who had got his start in the Hughes organization as a chauffeur for Jean Peters, the former Mrs. Hughes. Through their unflagging loyalty to Bill Gay, the potato-chip salesman and the former chauffeur had risen to directorships of a major industrial empire with salaries of $110,000 a year each, plus lavish expense accounts and bonuses.

Four doctors and a clutch of functionaries filled out the entourage. The doctor on full-time stand-by duty, a position he had occupied for more than ten years, was Dr. Norman F. Crane, a former Beverly Hills internist. The oldest doctor in tenure was Dr. Lawrence Chaffin, a noted California surgeon who had attended Hughes in his near-fatal crash in an experimental plane in Beverly Hills in 1946. Dr. Chaffin, eighty-three and independently wealthy, had come out of retirement recently to join the Hughes staff. The third medic was Dr. Homer H. Clark, a pathologist from Salt Lake City and the doctor who had headed up an extraordinarily complex blood-gathering program for Hughes. For a time, particularly in Las Vegas, Hughes had required periodical blood transfusions and had dictated meticulous restrictions on whose blood was to be transfused into his body. The fourth doctor, and newest in service, was Dr. Wilbur Thain, a general practitioner formerly in practice in Logan, Utah. He had disposed of a busy practice there and joined the Hughes entourage on a full-time basis. Drs. Thain and Clark were

Mormons, and each had connections with the Encino power structure. Dr. Clark was the brother of Randy Clark, an administrative aide to Bill Gay. Dr. Thain was Gay's brother-in-law, and had been a Chevy driver at Romaine before attending medical school.

Completing the entourage were five functionaries. They were Eric Bundy, who manned the telephone room, Gordon Margulis, Mell Stewart, Clyde Crow, and Jack Real. Crow served as a substitute for Stewart. Jack Real was "the airplane man," in charge of providing private jets for the entourage whenever it moved, or for incoming or outgoing Hughes executives from the States.

Margulis, Stewart, and Real were the odd cards in the palace structure that surrounded Hughes. All three were in the entourage, not by assignment from Bill Gay, but because Hughes wanted them there. They owed their jobs to him and not to the Summa triumvirate and were on a friendly basis with the billionaire.

Margulis and Stewart were close friends of long standing, although they had widely disparate origins. Margulis had come to the United States from London back in 1965 and retained a Cockney accent that he could thicken at will to total incomprehensibility. He had liked the States and had taken off on a wide-ranging, cross-country sightseeing trip shortly after his arrival. He had happened on Las Vegas and had been intrigued by it; a favorite uncle had been "the best tick-tack man"—a race-track odds signaler for bookies—in England. Margulis had taken a job as busboy at the Desert Inn without knowing what a busboy did, and had risen swiftly to waiter. He had been chosen for service in the Hughes penthouse shortly after Hughes's arrival because he was close-mouthed, polite, discreet, and hard-working.

Stewart was a Mormon ex-barber and male nurse, a typical "good old boy" with little sophistication and a lot of candor, and possessed of the shrewdness ingrained in many residents of small towns. Back in 1961 Hughes had lost the services of his regular barber, who had made himself *persona non grata* by telling a few innocuous stories about Hughes to a *Life* magazine writer. After an investigation, followed by a long briefing, Stewart had been chosen to cut Hughes's hair. Hughes had liked him. Like everyone who achieved personal contact with Hughes, Stewart was then co-opted into the Hughes organization and put on "stand-by" for instant call whenever the billionaire decided he wanted his services. He had gradually risen from part-time service to the position of a trusted functionary and full-time male nurse.

Jack Real was the solitary member of the entourage with any extensive business background. He had been a friend of Hughes for many years and was a former vice-president of Lockheed Corp., Hughes's favorite plane-manufacturing firm. Before Hughes went into his disastrous decline, he liked to talk about airplanes—old classics, his own planes, the newest jets—and Jack Real was an informed companion.

At least some of the Palace Guard looked upon Real, Margulis, and Stewart as loose cannon rolling about the deck of an otherwise tightly lashed-down ship. "They kept trying to drive a wedge between us," says Margulis. "They would run down Mell to me, hoping I'd complain about him to Hughes, and then run down me to Mell, and criticize Jack Real to both of us. What they didn't twig onto was that we would get together later and compare notes. If it hadn't been for Mr. Hughes, we'd have been long gone. But when we were off duty awhile, Hughes would ask, 'Where's Gordon? Where's Mell?'

"Besides, we did our jobs, kept our mouths shut, and tried not to antagonize anyone. But toward the end, I don't mind saying I got bloody well upset."

[ ]

The sudden move from Freeport to Acapulco had upset almost everyone in the entourage. The move didn't make any discernible sense. No one knew why they were taking the worsening Hughes to a Mexican adult playground, at least no one who would talk about it. To make things worse, no one in the group spoke Spanish.

The advance arrangements at Acapulco were made by Kay Glenn and Chuck Waldron. When the entourage flew in from Freeport, their bewilderment deepened. The tropical heat overwhelmed the hotel's air-conditioning and turned the Hughes quarters into a humid steam bath. The deteriorating billionaire complained repeatedly about the heat until the staff rustled up additional portable air-cooling equipment and put it in his bedroom. The communications system, efficient in Freeport, was uncertain at Acapulco. Sometimes Hughesmen would sit with a dead phone for an hour trying to get a call out to the States. None of the doctors was licensed to practice in Mexico, and the local hospitals were not equipped for any complex treatment. The Hughes group normally carried considerable emergency medical equipment with it, but there had been a breakdown in logistics this time.

"We all sat around and talked about how bloody awful things were, but nobody did anything," Margulis said.

"Until near the end of the stay in Freeport, Hughes had been eating better than he had for years. I'd got him back on steaks, making them into a stew, and had bought a whole tenderloin. For a while he was eating like a horse—for him, that is. Then in the last few months he slacked off and began starving himself again. At Acapulco it got worse."

Margulis and Stewart discussed this sudden deterioration. Stewart, who had some knowledge of pharmaceutics, wondered whether the "highs" that Hughes evinced, with the humming and talking, were induced by amphetamines. If they were, that might account for his drastic slack-off in eating, since amphetamines are notorious appetite killers, widely prescribed as weight reducers. If there was anything that Hughes, an irregular, finicky eater at best, didn't need—Stewart told Margulis—it was appetite-suppressing pills.

In the middle of March, Margulis was given two weeks off and flew home to Las Vegas to spend them with his wife, Pat, and his five-year-old son. He had been plagued with a gum infection in Acapulco, but the doctors had advised him to wait and have it treated in the States. When he returned to Acapulco, Gordon found Stewart ailing with the flu and diverticulitis, and *he* was sent to the States to recuperate.

"I couldn't understand why we were told to get treatment in the States, but Hughes was kept on in Acapulco," Margulis said.

Margulis returned to Acapulco in the last week of Hughes's life. He was dismayed when he saw Hughes again. In his absence, Hughes had somehow fallen out of bed and struck his head. The fall had sheared off a half-inch-high tumor that he had had on his head for years. The head injury had been patched up by the doctors without hospitalizing him.

Hughes was now terribly emaciated. Gordon sought out Francom and told him, "Something has got to be done or the boss is going to die." Francom was equally distressed.

"I told Mr. Hughes that I'd never seen him in such terrible shape," Francom reported. "I got no reaction from him."

Hughes had now stopped eating altogether.

"We've got to get some food into him," Margulis insisted. "Hell, I'll spoon-feed him if that's what it takes." He discussed this with one of the senior aides and "got a negative reaction." He said the aide told him, "If we start that, we'll just have to keep it up."

Periodically, Margulis would take Hughes some water and try to get him to drink a little, with minimal success.

"I got him to drink a bit of milk once, and I suggested to Francom that I try to give him some consommé. At least that would have had a little nourishment in it," Gordon said. Francom approved and Margulis prepared a small cup of warm consommé.

He took it to Hughes and found him in a period of lucidity. The near-deaf Hughes insisted that Gordon write a note telling him what was in the cup. Hughes refused the consommé and said he wanted "some dessert, to get my blood sugar up." He had liked sweets all his life and sometimes went for weeks on just candy, cookies, and milk.

What Hughes plainly needed, Margulis thought, was forced intravenous feeding, but not until his last few hours was an attempt made to drip nourishment into his wasting body. In his last three days Hughes consumed only a few swallows of water and milk and a few spoonfuls of dessert. "At least the aides *said* he ate a little dessert," Margulis said, "but I didn't see him do it."

At some point during his last days in the humid, blacked-out bedroom his kidneys failed, and he began to suffer uremic poisoning. For years he had been tortured by a severe germ phobia and had gone to fantastic lengths to avoid any possibility of contamination. Now his own body had betrayed him and, undetected by the retinue of doctors he kept on stand-by, was poisoning him from within. He long had been plagued by kidney malfunction; there were times when it took him hours to urinate. As the subsequent autopsy disclosed, his kidneys had atrophied to less than half their normal size and weight.

Untreated, kidney failure can kill an otherwise healthy man. Uremic poisoning was well under way before Hughes's doctors detected it. It showed up in a laboratory blood analysis, but there is a disparity in the accounts of when the blood test was run.

An Acapulco surgeon who served as a house doctor for a number of resort hotels, Dr. Victor Manuel Montemayor, was called in to examine Hughes hours before Hughes's death. He said he was told the blood test had been run three days earlier. But Dr. Chaffin, in the only interview he gave after Hughes's death, told a *New York Times* reporter that he ordered a blood and urine test the night before Hughes died. Margulis recalls it the same way. He also said that the urgent diagnostic test was complicated and delayed by the language gap that handicapped the entourage.

"When the doctors decided to run the test," said Margulis, "a Mexican nurse was called in to pick up the samples for testing. The blood sample, they decided, was to be identified as blood from Mell Stewart, who already had left for his home in Utah. They were following the usual procedure of never letting any outsider know anything about Hughes.

"They had a terrible time getting the blood sample out of Hughes because of his condition. His veins were shrunken and difficult to tap. When they finally got enough blood to test, his right arm was black and blue.

"Then they couldn't tell the nurse what they wanted done with the sample because she didn't speak English and no one spoke Spanish."

Finally one of the aides remembered that a man on duty at the Summa office in Las Vegas, John Larsen, spoke Spanish. Larsen was Chuck Waldron's brother-in-law.

"So they set up a conference call with Larsen, which took further time," Margulis said. "Dr. Chaffin was on the phone in The Office, the nurse was on an extension in Eric Bundy's telephone room, and they were both connected with Larsen in Las Vegas. The doctor would tell Larsen in English what he wanted done. Larsen would question him until he was sure he understood the instructions. Then he would translate them into Spanish and relay them back to the nurse, who was in the room next to Dr. Chaffin. When she had questions, she would put them in Spanish to Larsen in Las Vegas, and he would relay them in English back to Dr. Chaffin. Then they'd go through the same process with his answer."

The nurse finally comprehended what the Americans wanted and went off with the sample. Dr. Chaffin told *The New York Times* that he got the results back "at midnight"—less than fourteen hours before Hughes died—and that they confirmed his suspicions of kidney failure.

Medical specialists said later that the proper procedure would have been to put Hughes on a kidney dialysis machine. Ironically, his Howard Hughes Medical Institute in Florida had done considerable research to advance this life-saving procedure. But there was no kidney dialysis machine available at the Acapulco Princess Hotel.

There were other problems. A few days before Hughes's death, Dr. Thain had gone off to Florida. No one in the Hughes organization explained why Dr. Thain, who was considered the lead physician of the medical team, left his patient's side in his last few days. After Hughes's death, Thain refused to talk to reporters.

"Even before the test results came in," Margulis said, "everybody was asking what we would do if he died. But nobody said, 'Let's do something.' We had one meeting and tried to decide whether to fly Hughes to Mexico City, Houston, Bermuda, or back to London. But it broke up without any decision."

Sunday it was decided to summon Dr. Thain back to Acapulco. Jack Real was instructed to rustle up a jet plane, and the aides located Dr. Thain through his secretary. The plane picked up the doctor in Fort Lauderdale late Sunday night and rushed him back to the Mexican resort and his dying patient.

The final night was a blur of exhaustion for Margulis. "It was plain that we'd have to move Hughes somewhere," he said, "and that meant we'd have to clean him up so he wouldn't look so dreadful."

Hughes's hair was down to his shoulders and his beard was untrimmed and straggly. Neither his fingernails nor his toenails had been cut in years and were more than an inch long and curling in on themselves. His self-neglect was one of the closest-guarded secrets of the Hughes entourage. A sensational story had leaked out in 1971 about his bizarre appearance and had been indignantly denied. Twice since then Hughes had seen people from the outside world—Dictator Luis Somoza and the U.S. Ambassador, Turner Shelton, in Nicaragua, and Nevada Governor Mike O'Callaghan and gaming chairman Phil Hannafin in London—and each time he had been properly groomed. The stories about his unkempt appearance had been dismissed as wildly inaccurate fabrications. What no one in the outside world knew was that Hughes had been barbered and groomed immediately before these two meetings—and that the two groomings were the only two he had permitted in ten years. Now he was in a coma and unable to object.

"Waldron trimmed his beard short and cut his hair back to above where his collar line would have been. He must have scissored off four or five inches of his hair in the back," Margulis said. "I got some warm water and soap and soaked his hands and feet and trimmed his nails."

On Sunday night equipment for intravenous feeding was flown in from Los Angeles. The bottle was hung on a stand improvised from a floor lamp and the drip-feeding was begun. Hughes's right arm was so bruised from the earlier attempt to get a blood sample that the drip-feeding needle was put into his left arm.

At 3 A.M. Monday morning Margulis, who had been working around the clock without sleeping, fell into bed. At that point he still had not seen Dr. Thain.

Near dawn Monday, with Hughes less than eight hours from death, the doctors decided to call in outside help. One of them summoned Dr. Montemayor. He arrived at the Hughes penthouse at 6 A.M. He spent two hours examining the emaciated billionaire and later said he was "aghast" at his condition.

He was shown the blood analysis disclosing the failure of Hughes's kidneys, and his own examination showed that Hughes was drastically dehydrated, with a pulse so weak that the Mexican doctor could get no reading in several attempts to take his blood pressure.

The doctors explained to him, he told reporters later, that Hughes was a difficult patient, "that sometimes he refused medicine and food. And once he

49

had refused, that was final. Nobody could change his mind."

Dr. Montemayor said he would have handled things otherwise had Hughes been his patient. "Even if you have a patient in a delirium who rejects medical help, you don't take any notice of that patient's objections," he told reporters. "You administer the medical help. If I had been called into the case on Friday, I would have ordered his transfer immediately. It was obvious he wasn't getting the best possible treatment in the hotel. The best possible treatment would have been available only in a hospital."

Despite Dr. Montemayor's dismay at the lack of decisive action, hours passed before the billionaire was moved. To the very end, the entourage went through the old familiar rituals of secrecy, masquerade, and concealment. Before they removed Hughes, they reserved a suite at the Houston Methodist Hospital for him in the name of "J. T. Conover." They put a Houston ambulance on stand-by at the airport for an unnamed patient "suffering from diabetes."

At 9 A.M. an aide aroused Gordon Margulis by telephone and told him to come at once to the Hughes bedroom. He dressed hurriedly and went to The Office where he found a scene bordering on panic.

"Everyone was swarming around like a bunch of blue-assed flies, shredding papers and documents," he said.

He went into the bedroom. For the first time since the final crisis had closed in, Hughes was wearing an oxygen mask. It was connected to a huge oxygen cylinder Margulis had never seen before, twice the size of the stand-by equipment the Hughes party normally carried.

After a while word was passed to the penthouse that an ambulance was waiting. A guard was sent down to make sure that there were no onlookers around the ambulance. With this ritual observed, someone took off the oxygen mask so Hughes could be moved.

Gordon Margulis lifted the frail seventy-year-old billionaire, as light as a child, and put him on a stretcher. He and an aide carried it to the service elevator. Margulis raced back, wrestled the huge oxygen cylinder aboard, and Hughes was put back on it. During the descent, the elevator stopped with maddening frequency to pick up maids moving about their morning chores. Margulis stood at the elevator door, waving off the startled Mexican women.

They put Hughes in the ambulance and sped to the airport. Margulis and an aide lifted the stretcher aboard, and then shoved the oxygen tank on the plane. In their haste to hook up the tank to the oxygen mask, the tank rolled sideways. It was equipped with a water-level control. "Straighten the tank," one of the doctors shouted, "or he'll inhale water and we'll drown him." Margulis kneeled in the cramped fuselage and single-handedly rotated the huge tank to a level position. He backed out of the plane and Drs. Chaffin and Thain and John Holmes piled aboard. The door was secured and the jet took off, banking northeast toward Houston with the dying Hughes.

Back at the hotel the aides ripped the masking tapes from the draperies and let the sunlight flood into Hughes's bedroom. The layers of paper-towel "insulation" were gathered up and run through the shredder. The movie screen, projector, and amplifier were taken down and packed. There were no other personal belongings of Hughes to be taken care of. He had no photographs, no mementos, no favorite paintings, no cherished books, none of the sentimental impedimenta that people normally carry with them from place to place.

The man whose financial holdings defied comprehension did not even own any clothes—just a bathrobe, an old-fashioned Stetson snap-brim hat, a couple of pairs of pajamas, and a small supply of specially made shorts equipped with drawstrings. His long litany of taboos included shorts fitted with buttons or metal snaps.

He did not own any clothes because he did not wear clothes. For more than ten years he had shuffled about his blacked-out bedrooms naked or clothed only in his drawstring shorts.

[ ]

The decision to hospitalize Hughes had come too late; his heart gave out while the jet raced toward Houston. According to Dr. Thain, he died at 1:27 P.M., a half-hour out of Houston airport.

The news of his death was not announced by his doctors or by Summa officials. It leaked out to reporters from Houston hospital officials. For more than an hour after his death Summa officials refused to confirm or deny that Hughes had died.

This was not, in itself, unusual. The officials of Summa do not traffic with the press. They speak only through a "Hughes spokesman," a representative of the nationally known Carl Byoir public-relations agency. For more than twenty years the official "Hughes spokesman" was Richard Hannah, a one-time Hearst newsman from Los Angeles. He told newsmen only what Hughes or, in later years, the officials of Summa authorized him to say. Almost invariably he was not authorized to say anything. Newsmen who regularly covered Hughes came to expect this; when a story on Hughes broke, calling Hannah for his "No comment" became part of a necessary ritual. "In more than twenty years of dealing with Hannah," said one reporter, "I never got a paragraph of news out of him."

Hannah had died just a few months before the final Hughes move to Acapulco. The role of "Hughes spokesman" had been assigned to his assistant, Arelo Sederberg, a former Los Angeles *Times* reporter. Like Hannah, Sederberg relayed to the press only what he was told by Summa officials.

Within minutes after the first bulletin out of Houston, the phone lines in Sederberg's office in Los Angeles were swamped with incoming inquiries. In the first forty-eight hours his distraught secretary logged more than six hundred calls from newspapers, wire services, and television and radio stations here and abroad.

On the day of Hughes's death Sederberg was authorized to make two brief statements on behalf of Summa. Only one of them was true.

Summa finally confirmed that he had indeed died. This official confirmation did not wholly satisfy Secretary of the Treasury William Simon, who requested

FBI agents to take fingerprints from the corpse in Houston and check them with prints on file in Washington. The prints were lifted, flown to Washington, and compared with the fingerprints of Howard Robard Hughes. The prints confirmed that the body was that of the billionaire.

Late in the day of the death, Sederberg was authorized to state that Hughes had died of a "cerebral vascular accident," medicalese for a stroke. But the official autopsy attributed his death to renal (kidney) failure and said nothing about a stroke. The Summa officials did not reconcile this contradiction.

All other inquiries were turned aside. Summa declined even to identify the two doctors and the aide who had accompanied Hughes on his last flight. The press was compelled to report his death as it had reported his life, by piecing together bits of information from individuals who were beyond the control of Summa.

The off-the-record explanation for Summa's silence was that Hughes had been an unusually private man, and that Summa was merely observing his policies in dealing with his death.

This was the position frequently taken by his lawyers who would never produce him in court—that he was merely a quirky eccentric who put an inordinate value on his privacy.

The truth was that for more than a decade he had not been competent to make any sustained public appearance. He had been driven by private demons to the far edge of human behavior, where the line between sanity and madness blurs. For years he had lived in terror at the idea that someone outside his tight circle of aides and functionaries might catch a glimpse of him in his unnatural state. He had moved from place to place in a kind of enormously expensive private asylum of his own construction, a small little world where he made all the rules and everyone observed them.

Then he had lost control of it and had become its passive and willing prisoner.

[2]
A MASK OF SANITY

When death thrust
Hughes out into the world and revealed his true condition, the public reaction was one of shock and incredulity. How could a man of his vast wealth, with fifteen personal attendants, die in a state of malnutrition and gross neglect?

"Hughes would have got better care if he had been a penniless wino who collapsed on skid row," said a California physician. "At least some passer-by would have called the paramedics."

Superficially, his death fitted a pattern familiar to any newspaper reader—the wealthy miser who starves himself to death on a mattress stuffed with his cash.

But Hughes was no miser, hoarding money rather than spending it on food or medical care. The bill at the Acapulco Princess for his party's seven-week stay totaled $82,549, just for food and lodging. When the salaries of his doctors and attendants—from $20,000 to $110,000 a year—and the additional expenses entailed by Hughes's bizarre life style were added on, the cost of his brief stay in Mexico exceeded $250,000, an average of $5,000 a day. These expenditures were not unusual. In his last ten years, the cost of his traveling asylum and the back-up system for it ran to well over $1,500,000 a year.

Hughes died like a derelict because he hoarded power, not money. He prohibited his attendants and doctors from performing the normal services for which the rich hire attendants and physicians. The function of his court was not to oversee his welfare, but to execute his wishes and shield him from the outside world.

His attitude toward his physicians was that of a split personality. One half of him kept increasing the size of his personal medical staff, the other half rejected their services. More than twenty-five years earlier he employed his own personal physician—at $50,000 a year plus a generous expense account—but he rarely consulted him. As the years passed, he added new doctors to his entourage while growing more and more stubborn in declining their attention. He commissioned Maheu to employ one physician, Dr. Robert Buckley, and had him abandon his lucrative California practice and move to Las Vegas. Then Hughes learned that Buckley had received training in psychiatry and adamantly refused to admit the doctor into his presence. Psychiatrists terrified him, and with reason.

Hughes was a chronic hypochondriac who fancied

that he was beset by a variety of illnesses. But where the usual hypochondriac constantly plagues his doctor for new tests and diagnoses, Hughes hired doctors and then forbade them to verify or dispel his suspicions.

The tumor on his head, which was sheared off when he fell out of bed in Acapulco, had shown up back in the 1960's and had slowly grown larger. Dr. Chaffin repeatedly requested Hughes to permit him to remove it or at least take a sliver of tissue and run a biopsy to determine whether the growth was cancerous or benign. Hughes refused to permit this simple procedure and allowed the tumor to continue to grow. When the Acapulco accident severed it, Dr. Chaffin seized upon the mishap to make the routine but critical diagnosis. The test showed the tumor was benign.

Of all the professions, medical men are the least inclined to delegate their field of competence to their clients. When Dr. Montemayor, on viewing Hughes's deterioration the day he died, declared that he would have hospitalized Hughes much earlier, the Mexican physician evinced the normal reactions of a trained doctor. But Dr. Montemayor was not a member of the Hughes entourage and was unaware of the billionaire's jealous attachment to power.

His aides had lived with it for years. They rose to their elite status and survived there by their ability to respond to the wishes of a man possessed of a whim of steel.

"If Hughes told one of his aides to stand on his head in a corner," said one former functionary, "he would not ask Hughes, 'Why?' He'd ask, 'Which corner?' "

Kay Glenn, who wound up as overseer for the senior aides and the right-hand man for Bill Gay, attracted Hughes's favorable attention back in the 1960's, when Hughes was living in a mansion in Bel Air prior to his move to Las Vegas. The French Regency home at 1001 Bel Air Road perched on the crest of a hill overlooking the rest of Bel Air, which looks down on Beverly Hills, which in turn looks down on Los Angeles. The house was owned by a Los Angeles financier named John Zurlo. Hughes leased it through a Hollywood realty agent, Virginia Tremaine, who handled other property transactions for the billionaire. In keeping with Hughes's secrecy fetish, Ms. Tremaine refused to identify her client to Zurlo. During the years of Hughes's residence there, the payments for the house were always made by Ms. Tremaine and not by Hughes. Hughes insisted on this secrecy although everyone in Bel Air knew that Hughes lived there, and pictures of the mansion identifying it as his residence had run in both *Life* and *The Saturday Evening Post*. When Hughes finally gave up the lease on the house in 1972—six years after he had moved out of it—Zurlo said, "I still have no firsthand evidence that Hughes was my tenant."

One day at the Bel Air mansion Hughes observed that someone had dropped a bottle on a stairway, where it had broken and left shards of glass. The ordinary householder would have called a servant and had the broken glass swept up. But Hughes had a laser-beam attention that focused on small details, and an unreasoning terror of contamination. He was especially suspicious of floors.

Hughes delegated the broken-glass-on-the-stairway problem to his headquarters on Romaine Street. He described the problem and meticulously outlined the way he wanted it solved. The contaminated area was to be divided into inch-square segments with a ruler. He then wanted an employee to start at one side of this checkerboard and brush off and wipe down each segment, a square inch at a time.

The project was assigned to Kay Glenn. He equipped himself with a ruler, hurried to the Bel Air mansion, and removed the broken glass the way Hughes had ordered it removed. He did not see Hughes, but apparently Hughes saw him. Hughes later informed Bill Gay that Glenn was an admirable employee and that he was pleased with Glenn's stair-cleaning. Glenn soon began to rise in the Hughes hierarchy, by-passing functionaries of longer tenure.

Serving Hughes abounded with such incidents. He had an extraordinarily offbeat mind which, when geared into his phobias and his network of paranoid suspicions, propelled his aides into a Lewis Carroll world.

When he personally involved himself in a project, no detail was too small for his attention.

There was the Crisis of the Surplus Comma.

During his early stay in Las Vegas, Hughes departed from his practice of addressing the public through a "Hughes spokesman" and personally wrote several press releases. One dealt with what he perceived as a need for Las Vegas to scrap the existing

McCarran airport and replace it with one of his own design at a different location.

Composing the press release took days. Hughes drafted a rough version in longhand, had it typed, revised it, had it typed again, and continued this process in a marathon effort to get it precisely the way he wanted it. He finally achieved a version that was just right, except for a single flaw. It contained one sentence that he decided, after long study, had too many commas in it.

The sentence made reference to "Houston, Texas." Hughes remedied what he considered the surfeit of commas by taking out the one between "Houston" and "Texas." The final version was then typed and Hughes sent one of his aides to deliver the copy to the offices of the Las Vegas *Sun*.

He turned over the press release to Ruthe Deskin, executive secretary to the *Sun*'s publisher, Hank Greenspun. Mrs. Deskin, a veteran and competent newswoman, read the release and, on encountering the phrase "Houston Texas," put the missing comma back where it belonged.

"The aide became distressed when I put the comma back in," Mrs. Deskin said. "He told me that Mr. Hughes didn't *want* a comma there and that Mr. Hughes had taken out the comma personally.

"I told him that I could take it out, but it would just get put back in by the copy desk or the proofreader.

"This increased the aide's agitation. He was so genuinely upset that I felt sorry for him. So I resolved the crisis by following the copy through the newsroom until the plate went on the press without the comma."

Hughes's preoccupation with detail had plagued him for years. It was so intense that it immobilized him from other activities for long stretches of time. In 1950, when his burgeoning Hughes Aircraft was developing serious problems, Hughes addressed himself at extraordinary length to a crisis involving Jane Russell's nipples during the making of a movie called *Macao*. He dictated a memorandum that is a case study in compulsive meticulosity and a fetish for secrecy.

It was addressed to a man named C. J. Tevlin and was headed, in capital letters: IMPORTANT COMMUNICATION.

Like a CIA station chief briefing his agents on a top-secret project, Hughes devoted a full page to instructing his studio employees in how he wanted his memo about Miss Russell's nipples to be deployed. The memo was to be shown to only two trusted functionaries, who were to take his notes to the wardrobe girl in charge of Miss Russell's costumes. They were to remain with her while she read the notes, which were then to be retrieved from her and destroyed. Hughes stressed that he did not want any possibility of her inadvertently allowing someone else to see the notes, although he did not explain why such a disclosure would distress him.

He then went on for about four pages trying to explain what had upset him. In one of her dresses for *Macao*, he complained, the bodice gave Miss Russell's breasts the appearance of being padded or artificial. He was particularly distressed at several tiny bumps in the material near her nipples that gave the impression of multiple nipples, instead of just two realistic points. After an agonizing description of the problem, he launched into an equally agonizing prescription for remedying it, which consisted of a more pliant bodice and a very thin brassiere.

[ ]

The late Thomas Watson urged the employees of IBM to follow a one-word exhortation: "Think!" In the Hughes inner circle, where one advanced by sweeping a stairway a square inch at a time, and a comma could imperil one's standing, the watchword was "Obey!"

Hughes once acknowledged as much to one of his attorneys.

The lawyer urged him, in a telephone conversation, to take a legal course of action that Hughes was resisting. Convinced that what he was advocating was right, inevitable, and in Hughes's best interest, the attorney told the billionaire, "But, Mr. Hughes, you *have* to do it this way."

There was a long silence. Then Hughes replied frostily, "Don't ever tell me that. I have *never* done anything because I had to do it."

In return for anesthetizing their own will power and individuality, the Hughes aides were well compensated, and not only with generous salaries. The senior aides worked a two-weeks-on and two-weeks-off schedule. In their off-duty periods, whether in London, the Bahamas, or wherever, they commuted to their homes in the States by jet at Summa's expense. When they flew into Los Angeles for a conference with the Summa triumvirate, they were met at the airport in chauffeured limousines. At the resorts where they hid their employer they enjoyed saunas, masseurs, golfing, and tennis with what they termed "the power of the pen"—the authority to sign chits in Summa's name.

When on duty, they had a small fleet of cars at their disposal. Because Hughes was moved in and out of hotels and planes on a stretcher that would not fit into an automobile, he was transported in a common van, similar to those used by florists and neighborhood grocers for deliveries. The aides traveled in superior style. At Acapulco, for example, two cars were brought down by courier from the States to supplement the staff fleet.

Other than insisting that he hide in posh hotels, Hughes himself lived an oddly Spartan-like existence. In his latter years he had few options. A man who huddled in a blacked-out bedroom and panicked at the notion that someone might glimpse him from afar forfeits most of the pleasures of the *dolce vita*. But his personal austerity was of long standing and, at the outset, self-imposed.

He had little concern for what he wore even before he abandoned clothing altogether. In 1947 he showed up before a Senate investigating committee wearing an ill-fitting jacket he had borrowed from an underling. On another occasion he borrowed a topcoat from Dietrich, who was ten inches shorter than Hughes. It fitted Hughes like a child's coat, but he kept it for months. He wore shirts and slacks until they resembled something a thrift store would reject. When he ran out of socks, he went sockless.

The stories about his going about in tennis shoes and, in later years, shod in Kleenex boxes were unfounded.

The Kleenex-box story, one of the most popular items of Hughes folklore, grew out of an incident in the 1960's when a toilet overflowed in Hughes's bedroom. The billionaire had used a pair of Kleenex boxes as emergency "insulation" during the mishap, and the story had leaked out from the inner circle. It caught the public fancy and in the retelling became elaborated into a new aberration. Other than this one incident, Hughes never wore Kleenex boxes; when he wore anything on his feet, it was a pair of decrepit old sandals.

He was full of quirks about what he ate, but they were inconsistent and sporadic and had nothing to do with the refinements of the gourmet. There were long periods when his diet compared unfavorably with that of a social security pensioner.

At the Desert Inn, which prides itself on the elaborate menu of its Monte Carlo Room, he went for a marathon stretch subsisting on Campbell's canned chicken soup. While living week in and week out on a diet that a ten-cent-store clerk would have spurned, he was as finicky as a habitué of Maxim's about its preparation.

"It was not unusual for Hughes to take eight hours to consume the two bowls of soup produced by a single can," Margulis recalls. "He would eat a spoonful and then get interested in watching a movie on his projector—often a movie he had already seen twenty times. The soup would cool down and he would send it back to be reheated. It had to be heated carefully, so that it would be hot enough but not too hot.

"He would eat another spoonful or so, get involved in the movie again and send the soup back to be reheated. There were times when I reheated the same can of soup ten or twelve times.

"When he would get near the end of it, we'd have a new problem. He would have picked out all the chunks of chicken and want more chicken. So I'd open up another can of Campbell's, transfer some of its chicken to the chickenless soup, and then reheat the new mixture to the proper temperature."

While Hughes ate his canned soup in his bedroom, his aides and functionaries had elaborate meals sent in when on duty, or dined leisurely at the best restaurants and signed the checks for payment by Summa. Hughes expressed neither envy nor resentment at this topsy-turvy reversal of the usual master/servant levels of life style.

"In his last ten years he had no feminine companionship or showed any interest in women," says Margulis. "I never saw him even looking at any pictures of women."

He had abandoned his legendary womanizing fifteen years before his death. Again this had nothing to do with thrift. Much as he maintained a staff of doctors at his beck and then refused to call them, in the 1960's he supported a series of stunningly attractive protégées on an inactive stand-by.

In the Hughes empire, being put on stand-by by the billionaire was called "being on the hook." In the 1940's and 50's Hughes had an awesome array of women—some well-known actresses and a host of fresh young unknowns—"on the hook." For a considerable time he maintained five favorites in a kind of California-style purdah in a series of mansions. They were provided with cars and drivers, accounts at top-flight restaurants, and guards to fend off any trespassers, invited or otherwise. What they rarely had was attention from Howard Hughes.

In a remarkably candid interview one of them, Sallilee Conlon, told this writer that she had spent more than four years in expensive neglect, taking singing and dramatic lessons at Hughes's expense for stardom in a movie that never materialized.

"At the outset I saw Hughes every day for months," she said. "Then he installed me in a house in Beverly Hills and in the next four and a half years I never saw him once. Not *once.*

"He sent me flowers now and then—or at least had flowers sent to me—and that was all. I had a car and a driver and charge accounts. One day I asked myself, *What kind of life is this?* I called his lawyer because there was no way I could call Hughes, and said I wanted out.

"The first thing he asked me was whether I wanted any money. I told him that I didn't and he seemed surprised. Then I hung up and walked out into the free air."

Typically, Hughes maintained a security organization to guard his seignorial rights long after he stopped exercising them. This patrol was headed up by a man named Mike Conrad, who worked out of the Romaine headquarters. Conrad continued to guard the protégées for some five years after Hughes's attention had swung to other matters. Hughes's purser at the Romaine headquarters, Bill Gay, trimmed back on Conrad's budget and Conrad was reduced to staffing his "security guard" with amateurs such as vacationing college students and filling-station attendants moonlighting on a second job.

Their work was as undemanding as it was unrewarding. They also found it bewildering to keep surveillance over a collection of protégées supported by a patron who never turned up for any patronizing.

"I can't figure Hughes out," one of them complained. "He spends all this money on women, and he would make out a lot better and a lot cheaper if he would drop in some lively bar on a busy night."

The purdah guard was never terminated by formal order. In 1966, when Hughes moved to Las Vegas, Conrad grew weary of what had turned into a meaningless WPA-like leaf-raking assignment and quit. The protégées drifted off to wherever their talents and inclinations propelled them, with two exceptions who stubbornly and futilely remained in waiting and on retainer for more than ten years.

For all his Spartan personal habits, Hughes was one of the great acquisitors of our time. He combined this with a fierce proprietorship and an aversion to sharing his possessions with others or giving them up. He exercised this proprietorship over both people and things.

He left a collection of planes and automobiles, like his protégées, parked around the country under guard but forgotten and unused, their tires going flat and their motors deteriorating from neglect.

A California newspaper once conducted a census of abandoned Hughes airplanes. It counted ten—and missed three others that this writer had discovered.

This conspicuous waste testified to the diligence with which the Hughes organization complied with his expressed will, no matter how senseless.

"Once Hughes gave an order, it continued in effect because no one dared to countermand it," said Robert Maheu. "I recall that he had a small fleet of Chevrolets parked and weathering away for years at the Miami airport. We had a series of complaints from the airport management.

"One day I had them hauled off and junked. This set off a great flap among the Hughes executives. They agonized over what would happen if Hughes remembered the cars one day and inquired about them. I said, 'Hell, we'll just buy some old Chevies and replace them.' "

The organization that surrounded Hughes when he died was a product of necessity. It was distilled out of the Romaine Street headquarters where the peculiar disciplines Hughes demanded were ingrained into what became his inner circle.

Romaine was one of the oddest institutions in the modern business world. It comprised, from the early 1950's on, what Hughes termed "Operations."

The building is a two-story, fortress-like structure a few blocks south of Sunset Boulevard. Hughes acquired it in the 1930's in an abortive venture into colored motion pictures. When that enterprise failed, he used the building for a while as a storage place for his films. At its entrance is a small bronze plaque that bears the words "Hughes Prod.," for Hughes Productions, a long-inactive movie-making organization.

Contrary to many published reports, Hughes himself did not maintain an office at Romaine. He never had an office, in the conventional sense, anywhere in his empire. Restless, nomadic, and above all secretive, he moved about like a modern Scarlet Pimpernel, operating out of hotel rooms (rented under a fictitious name) or leased mansions (for which he never signed the lease himself) or out of automobiles or telephone booths. According to Noah Dietrich, Hughes never once attended a board of directors meeting of any of his corporations.

Given the extent of his enterprises, this unorthodox way of doing business required some central point of control. In the early 1950's Hughes designated Romaine as his operational headquarters and structured it to handle his executive eccentricities.

Noah Dietrich took up offices in Romaine and the building was staffed with a small pool of secretaries headed by Nadine Henley. The nerve center of the building was its telephone switchboard, manned twenty-four hours a day and seven days a week the year round. Under the supervision of Bill Gay, who received a giddying promotion from his position as Mrs. Henley's chauffeur, Romaine was staffed by a group of couriers equipped with a large fleet of Chevrolets. There was also a complement of limousines for the transportation of various corporate VIP's and high-level governmental officials Hughes courted from time to time.

Romaine freed Hughes to move about where his whim propelled him. Through its switchboard he could dispatch his orders to the heads of his various enterprises, either by dictated memo or by prearranged telephone conversation with his executives. He soon began to cut back sharply on the phone conversations and relay his decisions by memo.

Although his latter-day senior aides were basically adult pageboys, the executive heads of some of his enterprises were competent businessmen with minds of their own. They could, and often did, express viewpoints different from those of Hughes. Hughes viewed these discussions as an intolerable misuse of his time.

He resolved this by converting Romaine into a one-way avenue of communication. When the manager of Hughes Tool Co. or Hughes Aircraft called the Romaine switchboard, he would not be put through to Hughes. A polite aide would take the message that the executive had called. Unless there was something Hughes wanted to talk about, Hughes would ignore the message.

Since businesses cannot operate in a vacuum, Hughes's inaccessibility enormously increased the power and authority of Noah Dietrich. He was the No. 2 man in the empire and, unlike Hughes, visible and available. He was also a tough-minded and decisive executive. When a problem arose and Hughes was *in absentia*, Dietrich made the necessary decisions himself.

After their breakup in 1957, Dietrich frequently voiced an opinion that Hughes loyalists described as outrageous, treasonous, and tinged with blasphemy.

Dietrich maintained that it was he, and not Hughes, who had built the billionaire's fortune.

Certainly he contributed much to its amassing. The wellspring that nourished the Hughes empire was Hughes Tool Co., the oil-drilling-bit company Howard inherited as a boy at the death of his father. Hughes looked upon Toolco, as the company was known in the empire, as his father's success and showed little interest in its management. Although it consistently made money, Dietrich was appalled at its obsolescence and badgered Hughes to modernize it. He kept after Hughes for almost twenty years before Hughes gave in. Shortly after World War II, Hughes finally—with surly exasperation—authorized Dietrich to go down to Houston and "do whatever the hell it is you want to do."

Dietrich hired a production-line expert, Fred Ayers, who had engineered a new assembly line for General Motors. Without consulting Hughes, Dietrich spent $5 million on a modern production line at Houston. Within a few years the profits from the Hughes Tool Co. increased tenfold, to a peak of $59 million in 1956.

His profits from Hughes Tool were one of his closest-guarded secrets. But in 1972, when he sold Toolco to the public, SEC regulations required that he disclose this financial hole-card.

Between 1924, when he inherited the firm, and 1972 the company produced $745,448,000 in profits. The annual sales and profit percentages vividly reflect the results of Noah Dietrich's modernization. The sales in 1946 totaled $33 million. They rose to

$55 million in 1948, the year after the plant was modernized, and by 1956 had soared to $117,059,-000. In that year the company's profits hit a peak of $59,524,000—an incredible 51 cents of profit on each sales dollar.

The Hughes Tool profit-gusher enabled Hughes to build up TWA from a faltering regional airline into an international U.S. flag-carrier, and to convert Hughes Aircraft from a minor aeronautics company into the sophisticated electronics giant of today. Without Dietrich's Houston hat trick, Hughes wouldn't have had the money for these empire expansions.

Hughes's retreat behind the buffer of Romaine allowed his better executives to free themselves of his detail-meddling. After a period of futilely attempting to consult with him, they gave up, made their own decisions, and ran his enterprises as if they were their own.

The prime example of this is Pat Hyland, head of the giant Hughes Aircraft Corp. Hyland is respected throughout the electronics field as a superb executive. When he took over Hughes Aircraft in the early 1950's, the company was a shambles of internal dissension arising out of Hughes's notorious indecision. Its top executives, led by Tex Thornton, Simon Ramo, and Dean E. Wooldridge, had defected. Accompanied by hundreds of technicians, they quit Hughes and set up their own electronics companies, among them Litton Industries and TRW. The Hughes Aircraft fiasco was so far-reaching that the then Secretary of Air, Harold Talbott, flew to Los Angeles and personally excoriated Hughes for wrecking a major U.S. defense company and thereby imperiling the security of the country, Hughes Aircraft being the sole supplier for certain vital defense products.

Hyland took over the wreckage of the company and thereafter ran it as if it were his own. He swiftly replenished the staff, restored morale, and built the company to its present position as the nation's No. 8 defense contractor. According to company insiders, he did this without either interference or advice from Hughes. A close friend of Hyland declared that in more than twenty years as Hughes Aircraft's top executive, Hyland had only three telephone conversations with Howard Hughes.

Shielding himself with Romaine from the problems of his empire had other advantages for Hughes. When things went well with an enterprise, he profited from the success. When things went badly, the onus rested on the executive who had made the unwise decisions. Then Dietrich's telephone would ring and Hughes would order, "Noah, fire the son of a bitch."

"In the thirty-two years I was with him," Dietrich said, "Hughes never personally fired anyone. He'd give me the fire-the-son-of-a-bitch order on the phone and then become unreachable.

"There were other times he would give me an order he knew would offend one of his executives. Later he might talk to the fellow on the phone. If the executive complained, Hughes would pretend that I was the one who had issued the order. 'Did Noah do *that?*' he'd say. 'I'll have to straighten him out.'"

While serving as a shield for Hughes, Romaine was kept busy deploying his incoming orders and messages and catering to his fetishes. The office was stocked with white cotton gloves, purchased by the gross. Any document that was to be delivered to Hughes himself had to be typed by a secretary wearing white gloves, and hand-delivered by a gloved courier. This precaution had a medieval quality that contrasted sharply with the technological excellence of Hughes's mind. While newly purchased cotton gloves were probably clean, there was no assurance that they were medically sterile. And among the Romaine couriers there were cynics who took off their cotton gloves after leaving the message center and put them back on just before reaching their destination.

Although the Romaine switchboard was regularly swept for wiretaps, Hughes didn't trust it for what he considered important communications. He would call Noah Dietrich, give him a telephone number, and instruct him to leave Romaine and proceed to a public telephone. Dietrich would then call the number, give him the number of the public phone and hang up. Hughes would call him back and, satisfied that Dietrich had in fact left Romaine, give him his instructions.

Dietrich at that time was being paid $500,000 a year by Hughes. He was also nearing seventy, and the closest public telephones were more than two blocks from Romaine. But with Hughes the ritual of protecting his "secrets" was not a matter open to negotiation. The small stocky figure of the $500,000-

a-year Hughes executive trudging his way to a public phone became a familiar sight to residents in the vicinity of Romaine.

The orders that flowed through the lower echelons of Romaine were handled in a manner worthy of the KGB or the CIA. Romaine, like the traveling Hughes entourage that grew out of it, was severely compartmentalized. Hughes would dictate a message to Nadine Henley, along with instructions on what was to be done with it. The message would be sealed and turned over to a courier. Usually the courier would be given only the address to which it was to be delivered and a description of the person to whom it was to be handed. Sometimes this process employed what is known in intelligence circles as a "cutout." The first courier would be given a rendezvous point where he would meet a person who was either described to him or who identified himself with a code word. The courier would then return to Romaine, and the "cutout" would deliver the sealed message.

In Noah Dietrich's last year at Romaine, Hughes constricted his one-way communication lines even more drastically. By then he was telephoning Dietrich only sporadically. He invoked new restrictions. He instructed his staff that whenever he called Romaine, they were to discuss only what he was concerned with, and no one was to inject any other subject. In his memoirs, Dietrich says he received the same instructions.

"Noah, let's discuss only the problem I raise," Hughes told Dietrich. "I just can't concentrate on more than one subject at a time."

By 1957 Hughes was deep in a financial morass that was to occupy his attention for years. The development of the jet engine had revolutionized the airline industry and imposed upon it enormous new expenditures in converting from prop-driven planes. While he allowed his executives to run other branches of his empire without interference, Hughes had a jealously possessive attitude toward Trans World Airlines. "If Hughes loved anything," said the late Bob Gross, "he loved TWA."

His possessiveness toward TWA was complicated by a reality he had difficulty accepting. Unlike almost all his other holdings, he did not own TWA outright. He was the major stockholder, with 78 percent of its shares. But there were thousands of other investors who owned the remaining 22 percent.

With TWA, two deep-seated traits converged to impose stresses on Hughes. One was his indecisiveness, rooted in his compulsive entanglement with details. A man driven to compose a 2,000-word memorandum about the unsatisfactory way a dress presented Jane Russell's breasts was now confronted with technical problems of vast complexity.

The second source of stress was his imperious drive to get things done the way he wanted them done, and that way only. In converting TWA to the new jets, he insisted upon studying the plans, specifications, and performances of the various new jetliners himself. Then he agonized over his choice while time drifted on and other airlines, operating on an orderly corporate team basis, moved ahead with their conversion programs.

When Hughes realized that he was falling behind his rivals, he reacted with an almost manic burst of activity. He began committing himself to extensive orders with a series of plane builders.

One day Noah Dietrich sat down and drafted a résumé of the jet orders that had come pouring into Romaine. He was stunned by his figures. With engine replacements and existing commitments, the whole bill added up to $497 million. And Hughes didn't have $497 million unless he liquidated a huge segment of his empire.

The next time he talked to Hughes, Dietrich violated the new rule and injected a subject Hughes hadn't raised himself. He asked Hughes, "Where are we going to get this $497 million?"

Hughes insisted that he had not made commitments "for any goddamn $497 million in jets or anything near that."

"I've added it up myself, and I'll send you the summary," Dietrich told him.

"You can send me anything you goddamn please," Hughes replied, "but I don't owe any $497 million for jets."

Dietrich sent the summary to Hughes by courier. Several days later Dietrich's phone rang and Hughes was on the line.

"Noah," he asked in his reedy, plaintive voice, "where are we going to get this $497 million for the jets?"

The problem would have been manageable if it had been approached with a coordinated program. But whatever his other qualities, Hughes was iron-willed, secretive, and not given to coordinating himself with anyone. Besides, Dietrich had foreseen the problem of setting up a long-term financial program for the jet conversions and had showered Hughes with proposals that had gone unanswered.

In the spring of 1957 Noah Dietrich quit Howard Hughes. The immediate cause of the breakup was Dietrich's insistence that Hughes put into effect a long-promised capital gains arrangement for Dietrich's benefit. While Dietrich's $500,000-a-year recompense was princely by any standards, it was straight salary and hence subject to the highest income tax brackets. Most large corporations offset this with stock options for their top executives, whereby they are subject to the much lower capital gains tax.

But the Hughes empire was not a conventional corporation, and Hughes had a strong aversion to sharing his proprietorship of anything with anyone.

When Hughes commanded Dietrich to address himself to an aspect of the where-do-we-get-the-497-million-dollars crisis, Dietrich told him he would take that up when Hughes gave him the long-promised stock options.

Hughes responded with the reflexes his lawyer had triggered in telling him, "Mr. Hughes, you *have* to do this."

"You're holding a gun to my head," Hughes told Dietrich. "Nobody holds a gun to my head."

"All right, I quit," Dietrich told him, and banged down the telephone.

Within an hour, Hughes had a locksmith changing the locks on Dietrich's office at Romaine. It took Dietrich eight months and a court order to retrieve his personal possessions, such as his insurance policies and automobile titles. From that day until Hughes died, the billionaire never spoke or wrote a word to the man who had played a prime role in making him rich.

That same spring Hughes married Jean Peters, an attractive, dark-haired actress he had courted sporadically for years. He had dangled marriage before her but withheld it, the way he had promised Noah Dietrich stock options that never materialized. Miss Peters, a woman with a mind of her own, tired of Hughes's procrastination and married Stuart W. Cramer, a wealthy North Carolinian. Hughes assigned a Washington-based investigator to furnish him with information on the private life of Mr. and Mrs. Cramer. After a brief period Jean Peters and Cramer were divorced.

Two months after the divorce became final, Hughes secretly married Jean Peters in Tonopah, Nevada. By the exercise of devices available to a billionaire, the marriage was performed without the documents being publicly recorded in the names of Jean Peters Cramer and Howard Robard Hughes. The assignment of keeping his marriage license hidden was handled by a Los Angeles attorney, James J. Arditto, who later sued Hughes and collected an out-of-court settlement running into six figures.

By 1959 Hughes was beset by a series of new stresses. He had divorced his financial genius and married a new wife. He had lost the man who had handled his business problems and thus freed him to pursue his wishes and whims. In Jean Peters he had a wife who had said "No" to him once and was not inclined to accept a marriage supplemented by an array of concubines. And he was confronted with massive money troubles with an airline in which he had several thousand partners, in the form of minority stockholders.

Under these mounting pressures, none of which could be dispelled by issuing an order, or buried in a pile of $100 bills, Hughes's mind took an unseen curve and began to go round the bend. The world in which he had never done anything because he had to was turning unmanageable. So he fled it, and constructed one of his own.

He retreated to a pair of bungalows he had long leased at the Beverly Hills Hotel. He took up residence in one and installed Jean in the other. He summoned a small group of carefully selected aides from Romaine. Then he went into his first blacked-out bedroom, stripped off his clothes, and for the remainder of his life became an invisible man who operated unseen from behind a mask of sanity.

From that point on, his Secrecy Machine took over. He had been tinkering with it and perfecting it for years. Now he needed it and it was ready and operative, staffed by well-trained men.

In the everyday world, a recluse who cowers naked amid self-neglect in his bedroom is called insane. A billionaire who thus flees the world is termed eccentric.

This charade was played out by his aides for fifteen years. It succeeded because the truth about Hughes was confined to a tight, taciturn little group and because Hughes had stretches of lucidity when his mask of sanity stayed in place. Then he could confer with his lawyers and executives by telephone, or write his memos, and appear to be merely an odd rich man who preferred to function in peaceful seclusion.

But inside his hidden little world, more and more his mask began to drop away.

[3]
A $1000 HAIRCUT

One evening in 1961, Mell Stewart stood in the lobby of the Beverly Hills Hotel, clutching a small traveling case filled with brand-new barbering equipment. He was waiting for a man he didn't know, who was to identify himself with a code word. The man was then going to take Stewart somewhere to cut someone's hair. Stewart did not know who this someone was, or why the someone considered a haircut a classified project.

Stewart had been recruited for this mission by a man named Dallas Keller. Stewart ran a barbershop in Huntington Park. He was a devout Mormon, and his wife was the piano accompanist for Keller, a featured vocal soloist with the Southern California Mormon Choir.

"One day Keller took me aside and asked me if I would consider going up to Hollywood and cutting the hair of a very important man," Stewart says. "I said I'd be happy to do that and asked Keller who the man was. I was amazed when Keller said his identity could not be disclosed. Then he gave me my instructions about how to carry out this project."

In due course a man edged up to Stewart in the hotel lobby, gave him the password, and said, "Follow me." He led him out of the hotel lobby and through the lushly landscaped gardens to a bungalow. At the door he gave a coded knock—one rap, followed by four quicker raps, a pause, and then two more raps. It was a knock Stewart would use hundreds of times in years to come.

Stewart was admitted by a man who introduced himself as John Holmes. Holmes gave Stewart detailed instructions. He was to scrub up, doctor-style, in the bathroom before beginning the haircutting. Then he was to put on a pair of rubber surgical gloves. He was to have no foreign objects, such as pencils or pens, on his person. And finally, he was not to speak to the man whose hair he would cut.

"You can make signs, but you are not to say a word to him," said Holmes. "And you are not to tell anyone about this entire matter."

"The man whose hair you are going to cut," Holmes said, gesturing toward a closed bedroom door, "is Howard Hughes. He's occupied now. I'll take you in when he's ready for you."

Stewart sat and waited for several hours, his imagination speculating wildly on the reasons for all these James Bond–like instructions.

Finally Holmes said, "Okay, Mr. Hughes will see you now," and took him into the bedroom.

A $1000 Haircut

What he found stunned him.

"I'm a country boy," Stewart says, "and I expected that a billionaire would surround himself in luxury, with Rembrandt paintings on the walls and exquisite furniture.

"I found a skinny, bare-assed naked man sitting on an unmade three-quarter bed. His hair hung about a foot down his back. His beard was straggly and down to his chest. I tried not to act surprised, as if I was used to meeting naked billionaires sitting on unmade beds.

"I started to put my case with the barber tools on a chair. Hughes shouted, 'No, no! Not on the chair!'"

Hughes turned to Holmes and said, "Get some *insulation* for our friend to put his equipment on." Holmes got a roll of paper towels and laid out a layer on a nearby sideboard. The sideboard was already covered with a sheet, and so was the other furniture in the bedroom.

Holmes spread another sheet on the floor, and then placed a chair in the center of it. Stewart scrubbed up and started to pull on the rubber surgical gloves.

Hughes looked at him quizzically. "What the hell are you going to do with those gloves on?" he asked.

"I began to feel like Alice in Wonderland," Stewart says. "Holmes had ordered me to put on the gloves and not to speak to Hughes under any circumstance. Now Hughes had asked me a question, and I didn't know how to make signs that would explain why I was putting on the rubber gloves."

Stewart summoned his courage and broke the no-talking rule. "I put on the gloves," he said, "because Mr. Holmes told me to put them on."

"You can't cut hair with rubber gloves on!" said Hughes in exasperation. "Take them off."

"That's fine with me," said Stewart.

Barbering Hughes took three hours. There was a series of special procedures, which Hughes outlined in detail. Stewart was to use one set of combs and scissors to cut his beard, but a different set to cut his hair. Before Stewart began, Hughes ordered a series of wide-mouthed jars filled with isopropyl alcohol. When Stewart used a comb, he was to dip it into the alcohol before using it again, to "sterilize" it. After using a comb a few times, he was to discard it and proceed with a new comb.

While Stewart was trimming his hair on either side of his head, Hughes carefully folded his ears down tight "so none of that hair will get in me."

Stewart trimmed his beard to a short, neat Vandyke and gave his hair a tapered cut well above the collar line.

When he finished, Hughes thanked him and Holmes escorted him out. A few days later an emissary came down to Huntington Park and gave Stewart an envelope. In it was $1000.

He was told that Hughes was pleased with his work and wanted him to be available for future service. He was not to tell anyone, even his wife, whenever he was summoned for further Hughes haircutting. Stewart, in turn, was pleased with the pay scale as Hughes's barber.

Periodically, Stewart would be put on stand-by for a call. For holding himself in readiness, he was paid $75 a day. Often this stand-by status would stretch into weeks without climaxing in any hair-cutting.

He barbered Hughes a second time after the billionaire had shifted his hiding place to a handsome leased home down at Rancho Santa Fe. This time there were new routines. Stewart was picked up by Chuck Waldron and driven to Rancho Santa Fe, an attractive residential area inland from the ocean north of San Diego.

Waldron told him that he was to sit in the back seat of the car and not to get upset about his driving when they approached the Hughes residence. Waldron said he had orders to slow the car to two to four miles an hour, and that on reaching a designated spot they were to halt and wait until they got a go-ahead sign.

"They're watching us with binoculars from the house," Waldron said, without explaining why.

When they reached the spot below the house, Waldron stopped the car. "We waited," Stewart says, "and waited and waited."

"After a while I had to tap a kidney. I held off as long as I could, hoping the guy with the binoculars would decide we could come into the house.

"I finally told Waldron I had to get out and relieve myself. He got very upset."

"No, no, you can't get out of the car!" Waldron said. "Mr. Hughes gave specific instructions that you were not to get out of the car!"

"Then I'll have to go *in* the car," Stewart replied.

"Hold everything," Waldron said. "I've got a solution." He leaned over, opened the glove compartment, and removed a white canvas water bag. He emptied the water from the bag, handed it back to Stewart and said, "Do it in this."

"So there I sat, less than one hundred yards from a house with five or six bathrooms," says Stewart, "and relieved myself in a canvas water bag. Then I put the top back on the bag, and Waldron tucked it away in the glove compartment.

"Just then a fellow came out of the house and called, 'Okay, you can come on in now.'

"The fellow waited for us in front of the house," Stewart says. "He told me to be very careful walking up the steps and to go up the left side of them.

"I told him that I knew how to walk up steps. The fellow said, 'You don't understand. There's a dead mouse over on the right side of the steps.' He didn't explain *why* there was a dead mouse on the stairs, or why they were walking around it rather than removing it."

Again he was ushered into the presence of a naked, unkempt Hughes. Later he barbered Hughes several times at his Bel Air mansion.

Hughes's instructions became more and more bizarre. He had Stewart buy $88 worth of Nutrex shampoo, but then refused to have his hair shampooed with it. He allowed Stewart to clean his hair, after a fashion, with Minipoo—a dry substance used in hospitals on patients unable to shower. It is sprinkled on a patient's hair and then combed out.

Hughes also insisted that Stewart purchase new barber scissors each time and specified that they be made of German Solingen steel. He required three dozen new combs for each haircutting session and instructed that the scissors and combs be destroyed after one barbering.

In the meanwhile, Stewart sold his Huntington Beach shop and moved to Utah and opened another shop. A number of times he received urgent calls to come down to Bel Air to barber Hughes. He would fly down from Utah, be put up in the Hollywood-Roosevelt Hotel, sit around for several days, and then be told that the barbering assignment had been canceled. The Hughes organization would pay all his expenses, plus a generous fee—sometimes $500, once $1000—for his non-services as a barber.

In 1968 Stewart decided to abandon barbering and take training as a male nurse. When the Hughes organization discovered they were losing their barber, Stewart got an urgent appeal to fly to Las Vegas. He was installed in a suite at the Desert Inn under the name "Norman Cott" and was offered a permanent position in the Hughes entourage.

"I had expected it to be a weekend trip, but they kept me there for four months," Stewart says. "I telephoned my wife and had her cancel my classes at the nurse-training school."

Along with doctors he would not permit to treat him, Hughes now had a full-time barber he would not allow to cut his hair.

Although by the 1960's the outside world knew that Howard Hughes had become reclusive, no outsider and few inside the Hughes empire knew how deeply into seclusion he had gone, or the reason. The prevailing notion was that he was simply avoiding the horde of process-servers combing his suspected haunts in connection with the massive TWA litigation and other legal actions.

In 1960 Hughes had lost control of TWA when a consortium of banks and financial institutions required him to put all his stock in a voting trust they controlled. The following year the new officials running TWA sued Hughes for mismanagement. His Hughes Tool Co. countersued, and one of the longest, most complicated, and expensive legal battles in United States corporate history was under way.

David B. Tinnin, in his study of the TWA struggle, *Just About Everybody vs. Howard Hughes*, gives an overview of its dimensions:

The sums in the case were gigantic. All told, the claims and counterclaims amounted to more than one-half billion dollars. In addition, equally huge amounts were involved in developments related to the case. As a side effect of the events that led up to the conflict, a leading American planemaker lost $483 million in three years, the greatest loss ever sustained in so short a time by a United States business enterprise. As a highly ironic result of the suit, the largest sum of money ever to pass at one time into the hands of a private individual passed into those of the man against whom the legal action was directed [Hughes].

The amount of evidence and verbal testimony ran to incredible lengths. The documents numbered more than 1,700,000 single pages, filling 694 feet of shelf space. The pretrial testimony—in which some witnesses spent as long as three months on the stand—filled fourteen volumes, each thicker than a Manhattan telephone directory. Subsequent oral testimony filled another dozen or so such volumes. . . .

Arguing from diametrically opposed positions, operating on almost unlimited budgets, and aided by squads of assistants, the lawyers fought the case not once but twice through the federal judiciary system from district level all the way up to the United States Supreme Court. At the height of the litigation, more than forty lawyers and investigators were engaged in the case at a cost of $17,000 a day. The legal fees, court costs and sundry expenses themselves amounted to a considerable fortune—at least $20 million.

The TWA case set off one of the greatest manhunts of modern times. The TWA lawyers and executives desperately wanted to put Hughes on the stand, or failing that, to force him to show up and give testimony personally in a deposition under oath. This was not an unreasonable wish on their part. Hughes was the central figure in the case; he had run TWA with imperial authority, made all the major judgments or misjudgments himself. But just as the classic recipe for stewed rabbit begins "First catch the rabbit," to bring Hughes into the legal process they first had to catch him.

The intensity of the hunt was deepened by the outrage the TWA executives felt toward Hughes. From their view, he was holding himself above the law. *They* conformed to the requirements of the law, and they wanted equal application of it to Hughes. They had regular office hours, moved about freely in the open, and were swiftly subpoenaed by the Hughes attorneys. Some of them spent months being grilled under oath in the case by the aggressive Chester Davis or his colleagues.

Their bitterness toward the invisible billionaire spilled over in a court outburst by John Sonnett, lead attorney for TWA. He described his clients as "men of stature in the business world . . . rendering an important public service.

"I don't know how long men of stature like this are going to take this kind of abuse from a man who has been hiding out, apparently, in one or another back alley, garbage dump, a place in the desert, conducting his business in phone booths or men's toilets for the sake of secrecy."

To track down Hughes the Easterners assigned a young attorney, Fred Furth, and a seasoned retired FBI agent, Albert Leckey. The two men went out to the West Coast and hired a platoon of private investigators. They focused all the professional manhunting techniques learned by Leckey in the FBI, supplemented by a generous budget, on their search for the billionaire. Leckey let it be known, among journalists who specialized in covering Hughes, that a tip resulting in finding Hughes's whereabouts would be richly rewarded. Similar offers of cash were dangled before a few Romaine Street functionaries who were known to be unhappy with their working conditions.

To foil this manhunt, Hughes put Bob Maheu in charge of a counterintelligence operation. Maheu had considerable experience in cloak-and-dagger work. In World War II he had served in the counterespionage section of the FBI. At the time he took up the assignment of fending off the Hughes-hunters, he had recently come off a covert mission for the Central Intelligence Agency—an assignment that did not surface in public view until the 1970's.

In 1960 Maheu had recruited Johnny Rosselli and, through Rosselli, Sam "Momo" Giancana to assassinate Fidel Castro, his brother Raul Castro, and "Che" Guevara. The mission, centering in Miami, was intended to be coordinated with the Bay of Pigs assault on Cuba.

Rosselli has been described in a Justice Department document as a Mafia enforcer and one-time professional killer. Giancana was a stocky, cold-eyed Chicago mob leader with a file several feet thick in the organized crime division of the Justice Department.

The purpose of the murder plot was to wipe out the top three Marxist leaders of Cuba just as the Bay of Pigs assault hit the island. The plot was a classical CIA "cutout" operation. If the CIA-recruited killers were caught, the murder attempt could be blamed on the Mafia, seeking revenge on Castro for having shut down their profitable gambling operations after his takeover in Cuba.

Several attempts to poison and to shoot the Cuban leaders failed. The Bay of Pigs assault—because of inept intelligence regarding Castro's popularity with his Cubans, coupled with President John Kennedy's trimming back on military air support for the adventure—turned into a disaster.

Within a year, in 1975–76, after the Castro assassination plot was documented in a Senate investigation of the CIA, both Giancana and Rosselli were found murdered by persons unknown. Giancana was gunned down in the basement of his Illinois home, and Rosselli's body was found floating in a metal barrel off Key Biscayne.

Maheu's function had been to recruit the Mafioso killers, and he performed his assignment efficiently. He looked upon his role in the kill-Castro plot as a patriotic service for his country and "part of a military operation."

He has come, with the passage of time, to look back with less pride on many of the missions he performed for Howard Hughes.

"Hughes waltzed me up to the mountain-top and showed me the glories of the world," Maheu says. "I let all that money and power distort some of the principles I value."

Although his covert mission for the CIA failed, his assignment of foiling the Eastern Hughes-hunters was a brilliant success. While the Hughes-hunters under Leckey stalked the billionaire, Maheu and his agents stalked the Hughes-hunters. To handle this— and other increasingly important assignments for Hughes—Maheu sold his home in Washington, gave up his other clients, and began working full-time for Hughes. He bought and remodeled a handsome home in Pacific Palisades, and while it was being properly refurbished, took up residence in Brentwood.

One morning he observed Leckey cruising past his house. In frustration Leckey had abandoned trying to find Hughes and was now tailing Maheu, hoping Maheu would lead him to the billionaire's hiding place.

Maheu waited until Leckey had passed his house, then jumped into his car—a Cadillac equipped with *two* telephones—and caught up with Leckey and forced him to the curb.

He chided the opposing cloak-and-dagger agent. "Listen, Leckey," he told him. "Hughes owns 78 percent of TWA, and they're paying you, which means Hughes is paying 78 percent of your salary. He's a man who wants an honest day's work from his employes. So go and hunt Hughes, and stop following *me*."

Maheu resorted to considerable game-playing and feinting his opponents out of position. For several years the Hughes organization employed the services of a Hollywood actor named Brooks Randall, who bore a remarkable resemblance to Hughes. Or, more accurately, to what people *remembered* Hughes had looked like.

Through intermediaries, word would be leaked that Hughes had moved to northern California (or Palm Springs or some other once-favored spa). Then Randall would put in a series of appearances in out-of-the-way restaurants with enough ostentatious secrecy to attract attention. Leckey and his agents would thus be lured off to "tracking Hughes" for weeks in some area distant from his actual hiding place.

This ongoing manhunt, coupled with the fact that Hughes had not been seen in public for a number of years, attracted the attention of *Time*, *Life*, *Newsweek*, *The Saturday Evening Post*, and a gaggle of other reporters and photographers. They joined the hunt, and it began to take on the dimensions of a major safari.

The head of the harem guards, Mike Conrad, and

Hughes's double, Brooks Randall, were dispatched to construct a cunning artifice to mislead the Hughes-hunters and the increasingly inquisitive press.

Conrad took the Hughes Doppelgänger, Randall, to a remote wooded mountain area and set the scene for a picture. It showed the false Hughes seated on a rustic deck or porch in earnest conversation with several other men. The picture was shot with a telescopic lens, as if taken surreptitiously from a distance, but with enough clarity to bring out the strong resemblance to Hughes as he had been seen last.

Conrad then tried to plant the fake picture in *Newsweek*, using a woman friend as a sort of Mata Hari. Conrad had her approach Richard Mathison, Los Angeles bureau chief for *Newsweek*. Mathison was preparing a cover story on the Hughes manhunt for *Newsweek*, which was exhorting him to obtain a contemporary picture of Hughes.

Conrad's friend played her role well. She met Mathison several times in a dimly lit bar, gave him only a quick glimpse of the picture, and demanded $1,500 for it. "How can anyone find Hughes," she argued, "unless they know what he looks like?" Her story was that her brother was a Hughes pilot and had slipped off one afternoon and taken the picture from concealment. *Newsweek* wouldn't lay out $1,500 for the picture unless Mathison guaranteed its authenticity. He was reluctant to give his word on the basis of a glimpse in a dark bar. *Newsweek* completed its story without a picture.

The Mata Hari then attempted the same ploy on *The Saturday Evening Post*, for whom this writer was compiling a story on the TWA manhunt.

Aware that nothing regarding Howard Hughes was what it seemed, this writer set up a meeting with the woman and then had her tailed by a private eye when she left with the picture. She was picked up a block away by a car with license plates that traced to a Glendale rental agency. From the agency the car was traced to Mike Conrad.

Confronted with these facts, Conrad conceded that the photo of "Hughes" was faked.

At the time all this seemed just elaborate game-playing in a high-stakes legal manhunt. But it had a deeper and more desperate purpose.

The reason for trying to plant a picture of "Hughes" behaving normally was that Hughes was no longer behaving normally. He was not avoiding a courtroom appearance out of a cranky attachment to privacy. He was not capable of appearing in public. The tight little Hughes inner circle had tried to plant the fake picture of Hughes to conceal the truth about the billionaire. Like a puzzle within an enigma within a box, the Brooks Randall–Mike Conrad charade concealed a greater charade.

Throughout the years at the climax of the TWA litigation Howard Hughes saw no one except his immediate aides and his wife. He never once saw Robert Maheu, or the lead attorney, Chester Davis, to whom he entrusted the enormously expensive case, or his executive vice-president at Hughes Tool Co., Raymond Holliday, who was a defendant in the TWA suit, or his personal attorney, Gregson Bautzer, or his executive aide, Bill Gay.

Everyone presumed that these people conferred with Hughes frequently in person, a presumption his top executives did not discourage. Maheu had a convenient reply to reporters who questioned him about Hughes. "Those who say they see him, don't," he replied, "and those who see him don't say."

After the death of Hughes, Greg Bautzer gave an interview expressing his anger at "all those misrepresentations about Howard Hughes."

"Everyone said how long his toenails were, that his beard was down to his navel," Bautzer complained. "Let's get some of the misconceptions out of the way. For a start, he was always clean. I saw him over twenty-five years and he might not have been the most appropriately dressed man for the occasion. There were many times when he didn't bother to put on a necktie when he should have. But his hair was always well groomed. I've seen him with a beard, but a well-trimmed one. I've seen him in and out of showers . . . and I've never seen any long toenails on the man."

All of which was literally true at the time Bautzer knew Hughes personally, when they were squiring dewy-eyed starlets around Hollywood in the late 1930's and the 1940's. But according to Hughes's aides Bautzer never saw the billionaire during the final fifteen years of his deterioration.

Those who saw him indeed didn't say. During the TWA struggle they consisted of Roy Crawford, Howard Eckersley, Levar Mylar, John Holmes, and George Francom. The guards who manned the portals to his residences at Rancho Santa Fe and in Bel Air didn't see Hughes. Mike Conrad didn't see him. The bankers with whom he frantically negotiated for money to retrieve TWA didn't see him. Bill Gay didn't see him. None of his brigades of lawyers saw him.

Throughout the great court struggle Hughes huddled in his dark bedroom, running and rerunning his movies. He was now so fearful of germs that he would not touch anything handed to him by another person unless it was wrapped in Kleenex. He would not walk from his bed to the bathroom without laying a pathway of paper towels to walk on. He had gone for one period of three years without having his hair cut.

In this state of self-inflicted fear and neglect, the prospect of being forced into court or into a hostile lawyer's office was an intolerable nightmare. One can only imagine what would have happened to his lawyers' contentions—that Hughes was a proprietor competent to manage a great airline—if Hughes had come into court with aides laying a carpet of paper towels to the witness stand. Or if he had demanded that the bailiff wrap the Bible in Kleenex before swearing him in.

All that his attorneys knew was that he had issued a ukase—Keep me out of court. Theirs not to reason why. Thousands of hours of legal talent were devoted to combing lawbooks and precedents to convince the courts that the central figure in the TWA case should not be required to give his testimony.

In the end they failed, and Hughes suffered a default judgment rather than give his testimony. The judgment totaled $145,448,141.07. Although *The Guinness Book of World Records* does not include such exotica, certainly this was the highest price ever paid by any human for the privilege of remaining hidden in a darkened bedroom.

But even in his miserable isolation, he eventually triumphed. Well before he suffered this huge penalty in court, Hughes was forced to divest himself of all his TWA holdings. It was a stunningly profitable setback.

When the Eastern financiers wrenched control of TWA from Hughes in 1961, the stock was bringing $13 a share on the New York Exchange. Under the management of a new Eastern-appointed president, Charles Tillinghast, the company began rolling up spectacular profits. The stock took off like one of the company's jets and soared to a high of $96 in 1965.

Hughes was compelled to sell his stock that spring. He disposed of it at $86 a share. After deductions of brokerage fees, he received a net of $83 a share and was given a check for more than a half-billion dollars —$546,549,771.

He thus was forced out near the peak of the market. The stock then nosed over and, like a wounded bird, fluttered back down to its former level. At the death of Hughes, TWA was again selling at $13 per share.

There are those who maintain that Hughes, for all his mad behavior, was a financial genius. Dietrich, who knew him longest and best, argues that whatever Hughes put his hand to personally was soon plunged into chaos. Dietrich points out that the enterprises that flourished best—Hughes Tool Co. and the post-1954 Hughes Aircraft—were those that others managed without his intervention.

It is difficult to perceive any financial wizardry in

Hughes's great TWA coup. TWA was lagging dismally behind its competitors and was losing millions when control was wrenched from Hughes. He bitterly opposed the successful new management that put TWA spectacularly in the black. He fought off for years the effort to force him to sell his stock. He sold only when he had no other recourse.

His enemies prevailed and wound up with his beloved TWA. All Hughes got was richer.

In 1966, after collecting his $546 million windfall, Hughes made his famous "mystery" train trip to Boston. The gossip was that he went there for surgery at a noted clinic. Instead, his aides took over the fifth floor of the Ritz-Carlton Hotel and tucked him away in another blacked-out room. He did not go near any doctors.

He made the trip with his entourage, but without his wife. While his lawyers were unsuccessfully attempting to impose his will on TWA and the Eastern bankers, Hughes was losing a battle of wills with Jean Peters. He had decided to leave California, and Jean didn't want to go. He was a man who would not take no for an answer, so he went off to Boston alone. He had decided to move either to Montreal or to the Bahamas and went to Boston to ponder which place he would select. His train trip, he figured, would force Jean to change her mind. Instead, it effectively ended his marriage, although the formal dissolution did not occur until four years later.

Jean flew to Boston once during his stay there, for a visit of a few days. Hughes advised her that he had decided to take up residence in Las Vegas. She told him she would not live in Las Vegas. She then flew back to California and never saw Howard Hughes again.

Hughes refused to believe she would not change her mind. So he took another train westward, under intense security arrangements, and on Thanksgiving Day of 1966 moved unseen into the penthouse floor of the Desert Inn.

He was sixty-one years old. The TWA windfall had netted him, after capital gains taxes, approximately $445 million in liquid assets. This was above and beyond all his other holdings, his land, his Hughes Tool Co., his other enterprises.

A bemused investment counselor figured out that if Hughes had invested just his TWA profits in tax-free municipal bonds, he would have had a tax-exempt income of more than $26 million a year—or $73,000 a day every day of the year, including Saturdays, Sundays, and holidays.

The annals of great acquisitors abound with the stories of how, as they age and begin to look down the corridors of time, they abandon acquisition and try to do something socially useful with their money. Andrew Carnegie scattered free public libraries across the land. The Rosenwalds set up a foundation to aid the upward struggle of the blacks. Others endowed museums or art galleries or universities.

Hughes took his TWA cash and set about buying a whole set of Las Vegas moneymaking machines— the garish resort casinos. But again it was not money itself that he wanted, but the power money represented.

Las Vegas is a city where money makes the mare

go, and Nevada is a state fashioned for a man whose last and insatiable passion was for power.

Nevada is one of the smallest states in the union, in terms of population, and it is a one-industry state. It lives off gambling, and the casino owners are the major source of political power.

Until Hughes showed up, no person had ever wholly owned a major resort-casino. Hughes wound up buying seven.

Within two years he came as near to owning Nevada as anyone has come to owning a sovereign state of the union. He imposed his will on the legislature, the local governmental agencies, the state regulatory bodies. He bought politicians wholesale, and when he gestured with his hand, they jumped over his hurdles.

And he did this while lying naked on a worn Barcalounge reclining chair. By now he was so immobile that deep bedsores had developed on his back and lower shoulders.

Bedsores customarily afflict aging patients confined to convalescent homes understaffed or neglectful of indigent clients. Hughes developed them because he had given up sleeping in a bed. He now worked from his Barcalounge while awake and lucid, and slept in it when he tired. He aggravated the sores by insisting on sleeping on his back. "There was *no way* you could get him to sleep on his side or stomach," says Stewart.

He now not only stayed in his blacked-out room, he rarely moved from the old reclining chair.

Gordon Margulis worked for him nine months before he ever saw him. At the outset, Margulis's job was to fetch meals from the Desert Inn restaurants to the senior aides.

"The door to Hughes's bedroom was always closed," Margulis said. "One day I had delivered some food to The Office, and I was getting ready to leave. The bedroom door opened, and what I saw stunned me.

"There was this tall, skinny man with his beard down to his chest and his hair halfway down his back. All he was wearing was a pair of shorts. He was stooped and leaned forward with his long arms hanging down at his sides. His eyes were deep-sunk, and he looked like a witch's brother, if you know what I mean.

"He didn't say a word. He just stared at me, and then went back into his bedroom and closed the door."

Margulis was told he was never to mention to anyone what he had seen. He understood the implications at once without their being spelled out.

Just a few weeks earlier, the Las Vegas *Review-Journal* had carried a front-page story.

After considerable importuning on the part of Governor Paul Laxalt, Robert Maheu had set up an historical event. He had arranged a conference between the governor of Nevada and Howard Hughes. The *Review-Journal* topped the story with an eight-column banner headline. The headline proclaimed GOVERNOR TALKS TO HUGHES ON PHONE.

Margulis hadn't talked to Hughes. But he had joined a more elite group. Like Dorothy peering behind the impressive papier-mâché figure, Margulis had seen the real and pitiful Wizard of Oz.

A $1000 Haircut

After Margulis left The Office, Hughes summoned
the senior aides and questioned them at length about
who "that man" was. They told him his name was
Gordon Margulis, that he had been checked out, that
he was discreet, a good fellow, and a necessary
liaison man between the penthouse and the hotel.

From then on, Gordon passed freely in and out of
The Office. But so deep was Hughes in seclusion that
in the next three years Margulis glimpsed Hughes
only three times.

In 1970 Margulis not only saw Hughes. Hughes
spoke to him.

Hughes looked at Margulis and said:

"Hi, Gordon."

[4]
THE MAGIC
PHONE BOOTH

When Hughes arrived in Las Vegas on Thanksgiving Day, 1966, two uninvited guests were waiting to greet him. They were Nadine Henley, plump, smiling, her golden hair neatly coifed, and Kay Glenn, dapper paymaster of the senior aides and emissary for Bill Gay.

Hughes arrived at 4 A.M. by special train on the Union Pacific spur line down from Utah. His trip west from Boston had been plotted out on a logistic schedule as finely timed as the Allied D-Day landing in Normandy. He was to arrive before dawn, be transferred to a waiting van in North Las Vegas and whisked into the Desert Inn during the early-morning lull when the normally busy Las Vegas Strip would be deserted.

Between Chicago and Utah a crisis erupted. The City of Los Angeles, pulling his two special railroad cars, fell behind schedule. The Hughes cars would not make their planned connection in Utah and would arrive in Las Vegas *in broad daylight*. News of this impending disaster was flashed to Robert Maheu, who was orchestrating the trip from a post in Las Vegas. Maheu made a command decision. At a cost of $17,000, he commandeered a special locomotive, had the Hughes cars switched, and brought them into Las Vegas right on the button. The billionaire's invasion of the Nevada gambling center went off as planned, unseen and undetected by the enemy, which consisted of the press and the rest of humanity.

He was also not seen by Mrs. Henley and Kay Glenn. Disappointed, they returned to their Las Vegas hotel suites, sent word that they were in town, and awaited instructions. They did not have to wait long. From the sealed-off penthouse came word from Hughes.

Go back to Romaine.

They packed and went back to Romaine. They did not ask questions or request explanations, but they were disturbed. So was Bill Gay when he learned the news. During the years Hughes had holed up in Bel Air, Gay never saw Hughes, but at least the billionaire was nearby—a mere five miles away—and all the action was channeled through Romaine. Now he was 300 miles away, in the desert Sodom and Gomorrah that Bill Gay and Nadine Henley had always detested, with Maheu at his side.

They already were disturbed by Maheu's increasing authority and prestige. It had been Maheu—not Gay or his loyal aide Kay Glenn—who had been sent as the advance man to handle Project Las Vegas. From the Mormon senior aides at Hughes's side in Boston there had come discreet reports of a stepped-up communication flow between Hughes and Maheu.

Maheu had gone to Las Vegas weeks before the Hughes arrival with instructions to locate proper quarters for the billionaire and his aides, i.e., the whole top floor of a hotel.

Maheu had checked into the Desert Inn under the name "Robert Murphy." Hughes had warned him that the name "Maheu" was associated with Hughes, and using his true name "might tip off what I have in mind."

Using false names posed no problem for Maheu. In the FBI he had lived for two years under the cover name "Robert Marchand" while "baby-sitting" a defected French pro-Nazi spy who had turned double agent. But at Las Vegas the new name created difficulties for Maheu's young son, Billy, who readily adopted the identity of "Billy Murphy."

"I can remember that I'm Billy Murphy, Dad," he told his father. "But if I enroll in school here, you'll have to tell me how to spell Murphy."

Hughes was delighted with the way Maheu handled the shift to Las Vegas and the decisiveness with which he had solved the train-schedule crisis. He now assigned him a new mission—to buy the Desert Inn.

A legend has grown up that the D.I.'s owners, shortly after Hughes's arrival, had wanted the penthouse for the holiday influx of high rollers and that Hughes had snapped, "Buy the hotel."

The facts are less glamorous and more in keeping

with the real Hughes. Hughes had come west with the intention of investing a large segment of his TWA windfall in Las Vegas. Because of complex tax laws, he had to convert his profits from passive to "active" capital or suffer a severe tax bite. If there was a single threat that Hughes feared more than the sting of an unseen germ, it was the dread bite of a tax collector.

Although Maheu handled the negotiations with the owners of the Desert Inn, Hughes called the moves. He loved acquisition with the passion of a dedicated Monopoly player, and he fought for each Boardwalk or Park Place as if his survival depended on it.

The negotiations for the Desert Inn were complicated by its multiple ownership. While Moe Dalitz was the major point-owner, Dalitz had partners and every concession made to Hughes had to be a committee decision.

With Maheu as his emissary, Hughes began his favorite pastime of wearing down his opponents to compliant exhaustion. He would instruct Maheu to make an offer and get the Dalitz group to approve it. Then he would find a new flaw in the proposal and lower his price.

"I went up and down the elevator to the penthouse like a yo-yo," Maheu recalls. "I'd tell the group downstairs that it looked as if we had a meeting of minds, and then Hughes would raise a new obstacle. Five times the owners cut their price substantially before Hughes gave his approval. I went down and told the group that this time the sale would go through, and we shook hands on it.

"Then Hughes spotted a little item that displeased him. It involved $15,000 in a deal totaling $13 million.

"Several of the partners went up in smoke. One of them told me, 'We've had it with Hughes. We're going to come up there in the next thirty minutes and throw his ass out of there.' "

Embarrassed and exasperated, Maheu asked the owners, "Give me just one hour."

"OK, one hour," they told him, "then out he goes."

Maheu went back up to The Office, wrote a note and instructed Roy Crawford to give it to Hughes.

"I told him that we had made a deal and that I'd sealed it with a handshake, and if he didn't want to honor it, I was quitting then and there. I couldn't see him niggling over $15,000 when we'd blown more than that just to get him into Las Vegas on schedule."

Within minutes Hughes sent word that his attorneys would close the sale without the $15,000 discount. He also sent word to Maheu asking him to stay on because he wanted to talk to him on the telephone the next morning at 8 o'clock.

The next morning, Maheu has testified in court, Hughes telephoned him and in a two-hour conversation begged him "never to take that kind of precipitous action again."

"He told me we would spend the rest of our natural lives together. He elicited from me a promise that I would never leave."

Hughes shortly bestowed on Maheu the title of Chief Executive, Hughes Nevada Operations. Even that impressive title did not convey the true reach of his new power. With Hughes settled into the Desert

Inn, Hughes Nevada Operations *was* Hughes, and Bob Maheu now had the reins of the empire. His status was reflected by his remuneration. He was elevated to a princely $520,000 a year—topping even Dietrich's salary, which had been the highest in the history of the Hughes organization.

Moreover, he had the status of an independent contractor. Instead of going on the Hughes Tool Co. payroll, he remained as head of his own Robert A. Maheu Associates, with the Hughes empire as his client. He was not an employee on the Hughes Tool Co. organizational chart. Toolco merely paid him, and he was responsible only to Hughes himself.

Hughes's elevation of Maheu sent shock waves through the empire. The epicenters of dismay were in the cluster of Hughes Tool Co. veterans at Romaine and down in Houston. The Romaine center was now bypassed, its importance sharply downgraded. For nine years Maheu's phone calls had been routed through the Romaine switchboard, staffed by Henley-Gay loyalists. Now he was in constant communication with the billionaire, by telephone direct to the Desert Inn penthouse and by handwritten memoranda, carried back and forth by the Palace Guard. To further salt the wounds Hughes inflicted on the egos of his veteran executives, he designated Maheu as his official spokesman. The Byoir agency's Dick Hannah, who long had been "*the* Hughes spokesman," now became "*a* Hughes spokesman" who had to coordinate with *the* spokesman. In the finely tuned nuances of corporate power the change of a single word can create discord.

Bill Gay remained what he had been, a vice-president of Hughes Tool Co. But now he sat in isolation at Romaine with all the action centered in Las Vegas. He and his mentor, Nadine Henley, had ample reason to look upon Maheu as an ambitious ingrate who had somehow, some way, betrayed and undermined them with Hughes. Because of Hughes's passion for secrecy, they had no way of knowing that the downgrading of Romaine and Houston had been Hughes's idea, not Maheu's.

On elevating Maheu to the right hand of his throne, Hughes had instructed him "to keep the Houston people out of Las Vegas," except for their auditing firm, and to keep Bill Gay at arm's length.

Hughes later spelled out his reasons for banishing Gay from Las Vegas in two handwritten memoranda to Maheu.

"Re Bill, apparently you are not aware that the path of friendship in this case has not been a bilateral affair. I thot [sic] that when we came here and I told you not to invite Bill up here and not to allow him to be privy to our activities, you had realized that I no longer trusted him. . . . my bill of particulars against Bill's conduct goes back a long way and cuts very deep. Also, it includes a very substantial amount of money."

In the second memo Hughes wrote: "Bill's total indifference and laxity to my pleas for help in my domestic area, voiced urgently to him week by week throughout the past 7 or 8 years, have resulted in a complete, I am afraid irrevocable, loss of my wife.

"I am sorry but I blame Bill completely for this unnecessary debacle. And this is only the beginning. If I compiled here a list of the actions or admissions in which I feel he had failed to perform his duty to me and the company, it would fill several pages . . . I feel he has let me down—utterly, totally, completely."

Although Maheu eventually was toppled from power and replaced by Gay, he says, "That business about Gay being responsible for Hughes's loss of Jean Peters was a bum rap. During the time Hughes was referring to, he was still moving about. He tried to use Gay to tell Jean elaborate lies about where he was and what he was doing. Once he said his plane was forced down in the desert, when he was off somewhere else. Jean was too smart to be taken in by these stories, and that ought not be put on Bill Gay's back."

At the outset of Maheu's premiership, he took up residence in the former home of Dalitz, an elderly fellow whose early schooling had been in the Cleveland mob. Chez Dalitz was a sprawling one-story place adjoining the Desert Inn, furnished in what a visitor described as a "quaint contemporary Las Vegas version of classical Chinese pieces."

With Hughes's blessing—he helped choose the lots—and Hughes's money, Maheu built a $640,000 French Colonial mansion bordering the third fairway of the Desert Inn golf course.

Las Vegans, who genuflect to power while raising their eyebrows, promptly dubbed the residence "Little Caesars Palace." This was a double-edged reference to Maheu's new status and the ostentatiousness of the dwelling. It compared with that of a new Strip casino-hotel, Caesars Palace, which featured a restaurant called the Noshorium and a slot-machine arcade termed "Salon di Slots."

Among other creature comforts, the Maheu mansion contained a kitchen with five stoves, an open outdoor dining patio which could accommodate fifty guests shielded from the cool evening breeze by an invisible warm-air curtain, and a "communications room" with a movie projector, a custom-built sound system, and one of the first video-taping devices for recording television programs for later replay.

The single most important feature of the Maheu house, however, was a direct telephone line to the Hughes penthouse. Hughes could now pick up the telephone and talk to his new right-hand man without going through the Romaine switchboard. Could and did.

"There were times when I thought the telephone had grown to my ear," says Maheu. "One day I spent twenty hours on the phone with him. It was not unusual for him to call me ten, fifteen, even thirty times a day."

Could these conversations have been captured in a split-screen movie and shown to someone unfamiliar with the pair, the viewer would have assumed that Maheu was the billionaire and that he was talking to some scruffy indigent who had just had all his clothes stolen. Maheu sat at a polished desk in a spacious room with the ambiance Mell Stewart had envisioned for Hughes before he met him. A half-mile away Hughes sprawled in sad isolation, naked and scrawny, on his worn black Naugahyde reclining chair.

When he moved into the Desert Inn penthouse, it was remodeled to accommodate his secrecy fetish. The ninth-floor button was removed from the elevators that served the new high-rise addition. Only those with a key could take the elevators above the eighth floor. Directly facing the elevator door, when one emerged, was an armed guard at a desk.

The guards worked three eight-hour shifts, under the supervision of the day-shift guard, a barrel-chested, white-haired retired police officer named Pat O'Donnell. He looked like, and had the reputation of being, a man who feared no one except God and the Pope. He was an ardent baseball fan and finally, over the objections of thrifty John Holmes, had a small TV set installed on the wall so he could follow the fortunes of the Dodgers.

The guard's desk had two telephones. One went through the Desert Inn switchboard. The second was a direct hot line to the D.I. security office. It operated automatically when lifted off the hook.

Beyond the guard's desk, Hughes had a partition installed with a locked door. This served a dual purpose. If anyone managed to manipulate the elevator lock or acquire a copy of the key, he would be isolated in the landing space with the guard. The second purpose of the partition was to preclude Hughes's guards from glimpsing Hughes in the event he left his darkened bedroom. In his four years at the Desert Inn, his own guards, stationed only a few yards away, never saw their employer.

The only other access to the ninth-floor guard station was via a stairwell. The door was kept locked and the doorknob was removed from the stairwell side.

The eighth-floor bedroom immediately below Hughes's room was kept vacant and locked. This was to forestall any "enemies" from eavesdropping with special listening equipment.

The elevator guard kept a meticulous log of everyone who came to the penthouse floor, whether they were passed on through the partition door or merely delivering a package or message to the guard. The log noted their time of arrival, their identity, whatever they were delivering, and the time of their departure. Although there was fairly brisk traffic to the ninth-floor guard's desk, almost no one except the Palace Guard passed through the partition door.

The aides occupied the middle room of a three-room suite called Penthouse One. It had a door with a peephole grill. Anyone passed through the partition door had to undergo a second inspection before being admitted to The Office, where the aides were stationed. On the rare occasions when anyone was admitted into the locked office, the aides could alert Hughes so he could stay in his bedroom. Mostly he stayed there of his own accord.

Whatever his other phobias, Hughes did not suffer from claustrophobia. His bedroom was the smallest on the penthouse floor. It measured only fifteen by seventeen feet ("infinite riches in a little room"), considerably smaller than the usual "master" bedroom in a low-priced tract house. Even this meager Lebensraum was further cramped by stacks of newspapers and magazines piled along one wall.

To summon his aides he had a small silver bell, but he rarely used it. Alongside his lounge chair he kept a brown paper bag for his "contaminated" Kleenex insulation. When he wanted an aide, he snapped his finger smartly against the bag. His overlong fingernails produced a drumlike *whaap whaap* that brought an aide on the double.

When Hughes had concluded his instructions, or handed over a memo to be delivered, the aide left the bedroom. There was little or no camaraderie between Hughes and his aides, no "we happy few, we band of brothers."

"They didn't sit around his bedroom and tell jokes, or reminisce, or speculate how the Dodgers were going to make out," says Margulis. "Hughes didn't care for that kind of thing. Besides, there wasn't room. When members of his staff were off duty, he didn't even want them on the penthouse floor."

Except for rare occasions, he spurned his collection of hearing devices. "He could understand you if you stood close to him, face to face, and talked loudly," Stewart says. "But often he would say, 'Aw shit, write it out for me.'" On confidential matters the senior aides would write out their messages so they would not have to shout them, and thus disclose to others nearby what was going on.

His eyesight was bad, but he would not wear glasses. He used a number of magnifying glasses that he called "my peepstones," one of which had a battery-powered light for use when the dim-lit bedroom was too dark.

Surrounded by self-created disorder, he wanted certain things just so. He liked his documents neatly and precisely stacked. From behind the closed door of his bedroom, sometimes for an hour or more, would come a muffled *thump, thump, thump.* The first time Margulis heard it, he asked, "What the hell is that?"

"The boss is stacking his papers," the aide on duty said.

Later Margulis watched him many times. "He would take a thick sheaf of papers, whack them down lengthwise to align them, turn them, whack the topside, then the third side, then the bottom. Then he'd do it all over again, over and over."

When he wearied of straightening papers, or when his compulsion waned, he would pick up his yellow lined pad. Then he would write a message to Maheu about driving the AEC tests outside the continental United States, or picking a new President, or complaining that Nixon had nominated a new Supreme Court Justice without consulting him, or raging that the Justice Department was meddling in his casino buying.

Bob Maheu had a key that operated the ninth-floor elevator lock. Desert Inn employees grew accustomed to seeing him stride through the lobby, smiling and greeting them with a friendly "Howdy," then enter the elevator and rise directly to the forbidden ninth floor. They assumed that he went there and sat down with Howard Hughes to iron out the day's problems and tomorrow's strategies. From the Desert Inn word spread through Las Vegas that he saw the billionaire regularly.

[ ]

For their four years together in Las Vegas, Robert Aime Maheu and Howard Robard Hughes were the quintessential odd couple. Hughes had broken with his last prime minister, Dietrich, because after thirty-two years Noah had refused to bend to his will. When Maheu refused to yield to his orders in the Desert Inn negotiations and said he'd rather quit, Hughes cried, "Don't leave!" and named him to the coveted top position.

But when he had ripped his long relationship with Dietrich, Hughes was still mobile. He could fly about at will in his jets, play hide-and-seek with his enemies, rendezvous with his protégées. Now he was a skinny, naked old man bound by the chains of his phobias to a single dark room, shunned by his wife, and with no human contact except his aides.

Maheu was no Dietrich. Dietrich was a superb money manager, a good administrator, a top-flight organization man. But he was a methodical little man with no dash or fire.

Maheu had few of Dietrich's special talents. As a businessman, his own tax lawyer described him as a "walking disaster"—a characterization Maheu himself was fond of quoting.

"Most people, I have observed, spend 90 percent of their time scribbling notes and keeping records to justify their existence," he once said. "I prefer to use that time getting things done. I've never kept a diary in my life and I don't even own a watch."

He was a problem-solver, a man who could move a mountain (or drive a tunnel through it if it wouldn't budge), a high liver, a fellow who thought big instead of counting beans a bean at a time. He knew Presidents, waterfront bosses in the Mediterranean, and shadowy men like Johnny Rosselli. He made mistakes, kicked them out of the way, and forged on to do what he had to do instead of writing a memo about how it hadn't been his fault. He had a mind of his own and the juice of life in him.

Hughes plainly saw Maheu as his alter ego. Maheu

was the magic telephone booth into which Hughes could limp and then spring forth as the long-vanished SuperHughes. He could stride out into the world in the form of Maheu, deal with Presidents, governors, bankers, and Mafia killers, whisk himself where he wished in an executive jet, throw parties for ten or fifty or two hundred people without a thought of all the germs they harbored. He could saunter into the Regency in New York in full daylight without giving a good goddamn who saw him, and let a *stranger* carry his bags up the elevator with other *strangers* in it.

In occasionally blowing up at Hughes or arguing with him, Maheu was superbly playing the role Hughes had cast him in. To function as his surrogate, the Maheu-Hughes had to think for himself and speak out what he thought. Hughes's dark little cave was staffed with yes men with buttons to be pushed. Where they cringed at the change of one of his commas, the Maheu-Hughes could tell the Hughes-Hughes that he was fed up with his niggling over a lousy $15,000.

And along with all this, Maheu, like Hughes, wouldn't wear a watch. *Our finger to you, Father Time.*

Hughes's identification with Maheu runs like a leitmotif through Hughes's handwritten memos to him. Hughes wrote more than five hundred of them to Maheu on yellow legal-size pads. This writer has acquired copies of more than one hundred and has read some sixty more. Some of them came showering down when the convulsive split between Maheu and

Hughes breached the Hughes Secrecy Machine. Some have been published before; many have not.

Reclining on his paper-towel-insulated lounge chair, the billionaire wrote entire scripts for the Maheu-Hughes to play out for him in the exciting but fearsome world.

He once sent Maheu to negotiate with William Harrah for the purchase of Harrah's casino at Lake Tahoe. He composed a full scenario for Maheu, referring to him as "I" and himself in the third person. He instructed Maheu to "try something like this."

"Bill, I have to go to Los Angeles for a very important medical exam. I had postponed it to be free and to come to Reno and meet with you. But if you are not ready, I will go on to L.A. and reestablish my plans.

"Now look, Bill, I don't mind waiting another week at all and I am sure this is OK with Mr. Hughes. What has him upset is the fact that he is a man, like many you have met, who just cannot stand uncertainty. He has a number of other projects which depend upon this one. So, you see, his upsetment is not because of the delay, only the uncertainty.

"Now, you said this afternoon, Bill, that you wanted to present this proposal at a figure which will be immediately acceptable to Howard. Well, I think that is fine, and it occurred to me that you know in a general way what Howard considers fair. May I say to Howard before I go, that if he will just be patient for another week and quit fretting over this deal I am confident that when I return from L.A. in a week I will make one call to you and you will invite me to Reno.

"The main thing is, I just want to be able to tell Howard tonight before I go that he can quit worrying about this deal—that he can count on it and that you and I will work it out."

When Maheu did not come back as quickly as possible with his report on a project, Hughes would get anxious. "Let me hear from you, Bob. I want to know that you agree with me."

He was sensitive to Maheu's disfavor. "You have implied that all my apprehensions and restlessness and general calm-before-the-storm worried feelings which I have been experiencing lately were without any basis . . . You frequently get annoyed with me if I interrogate you in any way that might possibly be considered as an expression of uncertain faith and confidence. Now, Bob, I don't know if I can do anything at this late date, but I certainly think we both should give it an all-out effort. Why don't you work your angles and I will work mine and let's hope that between us we can accomplish it." The "apprehensions and restlessness" centered on a possibility that Arnold Palmer and Jack Nicklaus might not appear at a Hughes-sponsored golf tournament.

He tried to reassure his Maheu-Hughes that Hughes-Hughes was a pretty good guy. "My deepest thanks. You know, Bob, you told me that Harrah is the most undemonstrative man you have ever met. Well, maybe I'm not demonstrative either, but this does not mean I am not appreciative."

Sometimes he grew fretful. "Tonight I sent word to you that I hoped I would be able to reach you constantly throughout the evening. I was assured that this was OK. So under these circumstances, if I don't hear from you for the whole evening, I can get pretty restless."

He appealed for understanding. "The first thing I would like you to do in the morning is to read my last message over again and omit all of the exaggerated fantasies you saw fit to interpret from it. Just stick to what I asked you to do or not to do in the message. If you find any of these requests unreasonable, by all means let me know."

When Maheu asked him to send a little note to one of Maheu's aides, Jack Hooper, who pulled off a coup for Hughes while in the hospital, Hughes tried to convey his own plight to his alter ego. "I assure you, these rooms can be just as confining as the rooms of the Sunset Hospital."

Sometimes he poured out his anguish. "As usual, you fail to evaluate anything proposed by me in other than a childish light. I am getting pretty unhappy about your sarcastic remarks at anything I try to contribute . . . Some day, when you have time, just come out with it and tell me exactly and fully how stupid you really think your associate is."

He pleaded with Maheu, deferred to him, flattered him, and exulted when Maheu responded in kind.

"I used to be able to communicate with you and not be frightened for fear each word I spoke or wrote might be the one that would cause you to get angry with me and wind up with my stomach tied in knots. Please, Bob, let us go back to the environment of friendship that used to exist between us. That is all I ask. And if our differences are due to something I have said or failed to say in the past, or any other mistake I have made, I apologize most sincerely."

"I am simply delighted with what you have done about the Justice Department" . . . "I bow to your judgment" . . . "By all means do this. Your language is fine" . . . "I will continue to leave everything completely in your hands. If I did not have the most unlimited confidence in you, I would not say that."

"I am sort of anxious to know whom we are going to support for President and how much."

When things went well, he rejoiced.

"Welcome back! You may not be aware of this, but I have simply felt as if you weren't with me lately. It seemed that all we did was quarrel and bicker. Your taking hold of this bomb deal as you have (when I know it is not a favorite project of yours and you must be doing it in response to my request) . . . has meant a great deal to me. I send my sincere thanks. Also, I agree completely with every part of your plan."

Hughes tried to hold his Doppelgänger on a tight leash. Once, after a long stretch of twelve- to sixteen-hour days, Maheu took his family to Catalina Island on his boat for a weekend.

"We anchored," he says, "and I checked in with Hughes as usual with my location. I spent almost the entire two days at the island in a public phone booth talking to Hughes."

Hughes warned Maheu repeatedly not to let the old Hughes crowd "drive a wedge between us." When the construction costs of the Maheu mansion ran far over the estimates, Maheu told him what was happening and offered to pay for the place himself and take title to it as his own residence. Hughes already had a report out of Hughes Tool Co. about the overrun, sent to him on a confidential basis by a bean-counter appalled at the outgo of beans. Hughes generously waved Maheu's offer aside. But when Maheu moved into the house, Hughes sent a sulking note complaining that he had not been told.

After the years of desperate and futile concentration on regaining TWA, the project of adding Nevada to his fiefdom gave Hughes a lift in spirits. Most of his memos to Maheu were lucid, although they increasingly proposed improbably grand and delusive projects.

"More and more," says Maheu, "I found myself trying to protect him from himself."

Hughes embarked upon an intensive effort to bend the federal government to his will. The Atomic Energy Commission nuclear tests in Nevada infuriated and frightened him. He saw them as a threatening two-edged sword. The tests would scare off tourists from his gambling resorts and destroy his profits; they would pollute the air he breathed and seep their radioactivity through underground strata and poison the earth and water beneath Las Vegas.

Such desperate perils called for desperate measures. Twice he ordered Maheu to go to the President of the United States—first to Lyndon Johnson and then to his successor, Richard Nixon—and offer them one million dollars if they would move the test sites out of Nevada.

"Each time I went, because I knew if I refused Hughes would just send someone else," Maheu says. He flew to the L.B.J. ranch and met with the soon-to-retire President. Instead of trying to change national atomic policy with a million-dollar bribe,

Maheu expressed Hughes's "admiration" for Johnson and asked if there was anything the billionaire could do for him. Johnson said he was building his L.B.J. library, and the committee was accepting contributions limited to $25,000 per donor. When he reported back to Hughes, Maheu says, Hughes scorned the proposal with the comment, "Hell, I couldn't control the son of a bitch with $25,000." With Nixon, Maheu simply flew to Key Biscayne, spent a week relaxing, and then reported back to Hughes that he "couldn't make contact."

But when Hughes focused his rage on lesser goals, he frequently found political and governmental figures as compliant as his senior aides. The Justice Department under Lyndon Johnson had warned the Hughes organization that if he tried to add to the five casinos he had bought the antitrust division would restrain him. Nixon's Attorney General John Mitchell overruled his own division head—without consulting him—and gave Hughes the green light for a sixth purchase, and Hughes wound up with seven.

This federal about-face coincided with the secret delivery by a Hughes aide of $50,000 in cash to Nixon's close friend, Bebe Rebozo. Rebozo received two such packets of $100 bills from Richard Danner, a one-time FBI agent turned Hughes's casino manager. Rebozo said later he understood the $100,000 was a "campaign contribution." Instead of putting the money into any campaign, he claimed he put it in his safety-deposit box. He returned it to Hughes three years later when a swarm of IRS and Senate investigators began examining the money-passing.

Rebozo declared that he accepted the covert delivery of Hughes's cash without telling Nixon he had done so. He said he did not tell Nixon about the money until shortly before he returned it in 1973. Nixon supported this story and praised Rebozo as "an honest man."

But Rebozo, when he accepted the $100,000, was acutely aware that Nixon had been gravely injured politically twice before by a secret passage of Hughes's money. In 1956 Hughes had "loaned" $205,000 to then Vice-President Nixon's brother, Donald, in a futile effort to save Donald Nixon's failing restaurant business. The loan had surfaced in the 1960 Kennedy-Nixon Presidential contest and was revived two years later when Nixon ran against Edmund "Pat" Brown for governor of California. Nixon lost both races. Rebozo's attorney later declared that Rebozo felt the $205,000 for Donald "had materially affected the outcome" of both elections. For Rebozo to take more of Hughes's cash without informing Nixon required a political callousness and an arrogance toward Nixon uncharacteristic of Rebozo.

For Nixon not to have known of the $100,000 from Hughes until the spring of 1973 necessitated a conspiracy of silence involving not only Rebozo but also the White House staff that diligently monitored the press for him. Jack Anderson wrote an account of the $100,000 secret cash gift back in August 1971. The column ran in dozens of newspapers across the country and was spread over the masthead on page one of the Las Vegas *Review-Journal*.

There is no evidence that Nixon and Hughes ever met at any time, which makes their long, convoluted financial relationship all the more fascinating. They had striking similarities; each was personally secretive and addicted to deception, and each was lashed on by hunger for power. Nixon tended to equate wealth with respectability, and he looked up to and envied those who possessed it in great quantities. He was irresistibly and disastrously attracted to Hughes, who possessed more wealth than any other American. Hughes was much more cynical and pragmatic; he sought out those with power and offered his money as a fair exchange for what they had and he wanted.

Although Nixon dismissed the scandal of the Hughes $205,000 loan to his brother as a "smear" and a cheap-shot attempt to embarrass him with his brother's financial troubles, it was Nixon who sought the loan and, according to Noah Dietrich, insisted on it despite Dietrich's warning that it was political dynamite.

He clearly recognized the embarrassment inherent in covert money dealings with Hughes. When a Hughes underling, John Meier, became friendly with Donald Nixon during President Nixon's first term, the White House demanded that the Hughes organization keep Meier away from Donald Nixon. Nixon had his brother's telephone tapped, and Secret Service agents monitored him. Donald Nixon continued to consort with Meier, and Secret Service men photographed them together in Orange County. Maheu got a blistering call from Rebozo about the meeting.

Maheu had an assistant stake out the Las Vegas airport and caught Meier coming off the flight from Orange County at a time he was supposed to be up in Tonopah, Nevada. Maheu confronted Meier with his violation of instructions and gave him the choice of resigning or being fired. Meier resigned.

In addition to cozening Donald Nixon, Meier purchased a large number of mining claims for Hughes and was later named defendant in a $9 million fraud suit filed in federal court by Hughes Tool Co. Not even the severance of Meier from the Hughes organization deterred Donald Nixon from dealing with him. They later were "associated" in a Dominican Republic mining concession project that went nowhere.

Despite all this Hughes-associated trauma, Rebozo not only clung to the $100,000 in Hughes cash through the 1972 election, but fund-raisers for Nixon sought and obtained another $100,000 from the Hughes organization in the final week of the 1972 campaign. "They told me," says Robert Bennett, who succeeded Maheu as Hughes's political money dispenser, "that they had a lot of urgent last-minute bills for the Nixon campaign. Later it turned out that the Nixon campaign actually had more than a $5 million surplus. I was distressed at this news."

Neither Nixon nor Rebozo ever explained why the fund-raisers took a second Hughes $100,000 while the first $100,000 was nestling in Rebozo's safety-box. Nor did Hughes explain; one of the advantages of invisibility is that it exempts one from questioning.

During almost all of Hughes's stay in Nevada the governor was Paul Laxalt, who later became U.S. Senator Laxalt. Maheu became a favorite tennis partner of the governor, and Hughes was soon scrawling endless suggestions and guidelines and requests he wanted relayed to the man Nevadans had chosen to govern them. The Laxalt administration proved remarkably suggestible. The state gambling control agency waived most of their rules to avoid intruding on Hughes's "privacy." He was not required to furnish a contemporary photograph, to appear before the gaming board in person to be fingerprinted, or to provide a detailed financial statement. Once when he wanted a license in a hurry for a newly purchased casino, the control agency members, scattered around the state, gave their approval in a few hours by "meeting" via a conference telephone call.

Instead of slaking his thirst for power, the concessions seemed to make him insatiable.

In a deposition given under oath after Hughes left Nevada, his personal attorney, Thomas Bell, recited an astonishing litany of "missions" he had undertaken for Hughes. He said Hughes instructed him to stop a Las Vegas racial-integration plan ("Negroes," he wrote in a memo, "have already made enough progress to last the next 100 years"), to block the enactment of state income or inheritance taxes, to examine every bill in the legislature, and to persuade the lawmakers to adopt his views on what bills should and should not be passed. He was against laws prohibiting pornography, but wanted rock concerts banned in the Las Vegas area and did not want any streets "re-aligned" without his approval. Along with several dozen other concessions, he wanted one of his personal physicians licensed to practice in Nevada without taking any state examination.

In politics, both at the partisan level and in broad ideology, Hughes went where his needs took him. He had always been avidly anticommunist and wanted to prohibit any "Communist bloc entertainers or show" from appearing at any Las Vegas casino. Yet he threatened to join left-wing "ban the bomb" groups and spend his whole fortune halting the defense-oriented United States nuclear tests if the AEC continued to upset his composure.

In the 1968 Presidential election campaign he wanted Maheu to go sub rosa to *both* candidates and offer his full backing. His memo on Democrat Hubert Humphrey read, "Why don't we get word to him on a basis of secrecy that is *really really reliable* that we will give him immediately *full unlimited* support for his campaign to enter the White House if he will just take this one on for us?" ("This one" was helping stop the bomb tests.)

On Republican Richard Nixon: "I want you to go see Nixon as my special confidential emissary. I feel there is a really valid possibility of a Republican victory this year. If that could be realized under our sponsorship and supervision every inch of the way, then we would be ready to follow with Laxalt as our next candidate."

His very choice of the teeming Las Vegas Strip as a place to hide seemed schizoid. The Desert Inn was hardly a Walden Pond. Las Vegas attracts millions of tourists a year, and because Hughes concealed himself there, the Desert Inn became a special point of interest that outdrew Hoover Dam. His figurative shouts of "Go away!" fetched throngs to ask what all the shouting was about. From the D.I. poolside, ground-floor patios, and high-rise balconies, and from adjoining hotels, hundreds of binoculars trained on the draperies of the penthouse. If the gambling tables palled, there was always the exciting game of trying to catch a glimpse of Hughes. "Seeing" Hughes became a Las Vegas cachet, like rolling fifteen straight passes at a crap table.

So many people "saw" Hughes that sightings lost their value. One had to "talk" to him to achieve distinction, or pick him up at the roadside and lend him a quarter, as a Utah filling station owner, Melvin Dummar, claimed to have done.

The lesser rich, even mere millionaires, have no problems buying privacy. There are men with fortunes in nine figures almost no one in the United States has ever heard of. No throngs pace the grounds of the Rockefeller residences at Pocantico. Hughes could have purchased his own island in a wilderness and fenced it in for what it cost him to maintain his secret enclave two or three months atop the busy Desert Inn.

Las Vegas treated him like some valuable asset rather than a man who was behaving with curious contradictions. Hank Greenspun, editor-publisher of the Las Vegas *Sun* and an inveterate journalistic boat-rocker, put a WELCOME TO LAS VEGAS editorial on the front page and cautioned newsmen against disturbing Hughes's privacy. Governor Laxalt exulted that Hughes had put a Good Housekeeping Seal of Approval on Las Vegas gambling and had exorcized the last ghosts of the bad old mobster days. The usually savvy New York *Daily News* did a feature story suggesting that Hughes had gone to Las Vegas to drive out organized crime.

Hughes did indeed upgrade Las Vegas, if one

measures civic improvement with a cash register. Land prices along the Strip doubled, tripled, quadrupled. When the legislature changed the rules and approved corporate ownership of casinos, to accommodate Hughes Tool Co.'s multiple ownership, other corporations moved in and went into the gambling business. Hughes, however, did not welcome the boom he was praised for generating. He wrote memo after memo constructing scenarios for blocking, discouraging, sabotaging new rivals—without reconciling his actions with his long-proclaimed admiration for free enterprise.

None of this surfaced at the time. With Maheu muffling Hughes's *outré* power-madness and the Palace Guard keeping him invisible, Las Vegas hailed him as a sort of real-life Daddy Warbucks with a few odd habits. From time to time, however, Maheu sensed something askew with Hughes. "He would start repeating himself on the telephone now and then," Maheu says. "He would say the same thing over and over, obviously unaware that he was talking like a stuck record. Then there would be sudden periods of total silence when he wouldn't call, or respond to memos."

In one memo Hughes glimpsed that his own mind was not functioning properly. He wrote: "Bob, I have only three really serious problems that might prevent an activation of the mining properties, the new hotels, the automobile race track, and even a few more Nevada projects . . . These three are: 1. The new Showboat. 2. The race-track legislation which must have the most immediate attention.

"Bob, I know this sounds odd, but I cannot remember the 3rd item. It is equally important with the other 2. So that makes it even more surprising that I have forgotten it. However, I will remember it very soon and convey it to you just the minute my brain starts to work."

Maheu never did learn that third "really serious" problem that was bothering Hughes.

But there were more than three, and up in the penthouse, behind their two locked barriers, the inner circle of aides was trying to cope with them daily.

[5]
SOME ICE CREAM
FOR MR. HUGHES

He had a new compulsion. He would sit in his bathroom or on his lounge chair and lave his hands and upper arms over and over with alcohol. Like Lady Macbeth's "damned spot," whatever he was trying to cleanse away would not out. He would wash and wash, the alcohol dripping down and turning his paper-towel "insulation" into a sodden pulp. When he gave up, the paper towels would be gathered up and a fresh paper carpet laid down. The towels were then run through a shredder.

Mell Stewart was assigned the job of procuring the alcohol. "He used the same kind of hospital alcohol that he made me use for comb-dipping when I'd cut his hair," Stewart says. There were precautions to be taken, convolutions to be followed. One didn't just requisition a gallon, or five gallons, of alcohol and have it delivered to the Desert Inn.

Stewart was instructed to purchase the alcohol a few bottles at a time at Las Vegas drugstores.

"I was told to buy it secretly," Stewart says. "I was told never to identify myself, either by name or as an employee of the Hughes organization. If the clerk expressed any curiosity about the size of the purchase or the frequency of my visits, I was to scratch that drugstore off my list and never go back there.

"I bought alcohol all over Las Vegas, North Las Vegas, even out in Henderson and Boulder. I'd buy six, eight bottles at a time. I don't know what the clerks thought. Hospitals and convalescent homes buy the stuff wholesale. Maybe they thought I was some kind of mad scientist."

Stewart was housed at the Desert Inn in quarters paid for by the Hughes organization. Theoretically he was the stand-by-barber, but Hughes was again letting his hair and beard grow untended.

The Hughes inner circle had several crises with stand-by personnel who had to be on call but were never called. One of the doctors, with nothing to do but stay by the telephone for a summons that didn't come, turned into an alcoholic. Then twice, when Hughes required blood transfusions, the doctor was so shaky he couldn't perform this simple procedure. The only other doctor available was the one with psychiatric training, and he had been banned by Hughes from ever approaching him.

Twice an outside doctor had to be brought in. To

contain this new breach in Hughes's privacy, both times the same physician, Dr. Harold Feikes, was used.

Stewart was an energetic fellow who couldn't sit in a room for three or four years waiting to give Hughes a haircut. So the aides found things for him to do. In addition to serving as Hughes's secret "connection" to obtain hospital alcohol, he was assigned to clip news stories out of the Las Vegas papers and *The Wall Street Journal*, to collect the mail, and to dispose of the "burn bags."

The internal Summa-Hughes mail did not go through the Desert Inn, where some clever enemy might infiltrate an agent and intercept it. It was mailed instead to a special box maintained at the McCarran Airport postal substation, where Stewart picked it up daily.

The Office was equipped with a document shredder, similar to those used at the Pentagon, the State Department, Richard Nixon's campaign re-election office, and other establishments with secrets to guard. All discarded papers, plus the alcohol-soaked paper towels, were run through the shredder and tucked into plastic bags and sealed.

Behind the Desert Inn was a gas-fired outdoor incinerator for burning the hotel's rubbish. Each day when it was fired up, Stewart would take the thoroughly shredded papers down and throw them into the incinerator. He was instructed to stay at the incinerator and personally verify that the shreds were reduced to ashes.

Feeding Hughes was a constant problem and a

periodic crisis. When he came off his marathon canned-chicken-soup diet, he switched to the hotel's vegetable soup.

"Now, this is only a trial period," Hughes said, "because I want it just the way I like it, and it has to be right."

Hughes instructed that his soup be prepared separately from that for hotel diners. It was to be cooked only in a stainless steel pot and with bottled Poland water.

He tried the vegetable soup three times, labeling them Batch One, Two, and Three, and then designated one of the batches as acceptable.

"The chef told me later," says Margulis, "that he had used the same recipe each time."

One day while watching television, Hughes saw a commercial for TV frozen dinners and decided to try them. He liked Swanson's frozen turkey dinners and abandoned his soup diet. For weeks, day in and day out, he lived on the kind of fast food that housewives resort to in emergencies.

The Swanson TV turkey dinners were fine, Hughes pronounced, but there were two drawbacks. They contained a mixture of white and dark meat. Hughes preferred all white. The turkey dinners had apple cobbler, and some of the other frozen dinners he had tried had peach cobbler. Hughes wanted peach cobbler with his turkey. He told his aides to call the Swanson people and inform them of his preferences.

"Have them switch the peach cobbler to the turkey dinner and take out the dark meat," said the billionaire.

This order was solemnly handed on to Gordon Margulis.

"You're pulling my leg," said Margulis, then new to the world of Howard Hughes.

"No, no," said the aide. "Those are Mr. Hughes's instructions."

"You can't have a company that turns out frozen dinners by the millions whip up a few special orders every week for *one customer*," Margulis complained.

"*Call* them," the aide said.

"We were rescued from this because Hughes discovered Arby's sandwiches," Margulis says. "Arby" (for Roast Reef) is a Western fast-food chain. Hughes, who watched a lot of television at Las Vegas, learned about Arby's through a TV commercial.

He decided to try them, but he had some stipulations. He wanted the local Arby shop to obtain a special stainless steel blade, to be used only for slicing beef for the Hughes sandwiches. He would try two Arby's, and if he liked them he would continue his patronage.

"I went down and walked around the D.I. pool a few times and tried to figure out how to handle this," Margulis says. "I was afraid to fake it and just get a couple of plain Arby's, the kind everybody else ate, because the Old Man had a way of checking up on whether his orders were followed. If you got caught cutting corners, there was hell to pay."

Margulis went back to The Office and stalled for time. He reported that the Arby people didn't know whether they could find a special stainless steel cutting wheel. Then Hughes inexplicably abandoned his fast-food diet and switched to filet mignon. And not just any filet.

"He wanted them very small and very thin—one-half of a filet slice about a quarter-inch thick—and they had to be round," Margulis says. "He liked them well done. He ate them with peas, baby carrots and diced boiled potatoes—day after day after day.

"He didn't want the filet cooked in the penthouse —which had a little kitchen—because he said the cooking would pollute his air. He also wanted the peas to be the small young ones."

Hughes's aversion to large peas was one of his lesser quirks but it was of long duration. For some reason he had disliked large peas all his life. Noah Dietrich remembered dining with Hughes and Hughes's first wife, the former Ella Rice, in Los Angeles back in the 30's. He said Hughes had a small silver rakelike device and would rake the peas on his plate. Those too large to pass through the rake were isolated and went uneaten.

"One day Hughes learned that a man called Pancho was the maitre d' at the Desert Inn," says Margulis. "He said he thought he was the same Pancho who worked years ago at a place in Beverly Hills."

"Tell him I'd like that special mustard sauce he used to make for me," Hughes ordered.

"He had a remarkable memory about some things," Margulis. So, fortunately, did Pancho. He remembered the formula for the mustard sauce and whipped up a batch. It was fashioned from Coleman's powdered mustard, Lea and Perrin's Sauce, thick brown gravy, and a dash of butter. Hughes liked it very hot in a side dish with his filets.

Margulis was pleased when Hughes ate. When he grew despondent, he would go without any food. His weight was far below normal, about 130 pounds, even when he was eating regularly. When he skipped meals, it dropped sharply.

For months he would demand the same meal every day. This precipitated the great Baskin-Robbins ice-cream fiasco.

He tried some of Baskin-Robbins' thirty-one varieties of ice cream, chose banana-nut as his favorite, and had two scoops of it with every meal for months. The staff bought it in large containers and kept it constantly on hand.

One day the ice-cream supply was running low, and Mell Stewart was sent to the local Baskin-Robbins to replenish it. He came back with bleak news. The ice-cream chain, which adds new varieties periodically and drops others, had discontinued the Hughes favorite. No more banana-nut. The aides went into a panic. There were only about six or eight scoops left, and then what?

One of the aides saw a way out of the looming crisis. He told Stewart to telephone the Baskin-Robbins office in California and ask if they could make up a special batch of banana-nut.

"I got on the telephone and talked to one of the executives," Stewart says. "Without telling him the cause of the problem, I asked him if the company could make up a discontinued flavor on special order.

"He said they didn't ordinarily do this, but it could be done.

"I asked what was the smallest batch they could make on special order. He said 350 gallons."

Stewart's mind reeled. He couldn't even envision what 350 gallons of ice cream looked like. But he *could* picture what the penthouse would look like if he came back and said, "No banana-nut."

"By now I was beginning to understand how things worked in the Hughes organization," Stewart says. "You did what you had to do. So I took a deep breath and told him to make up the batch at once."

The ice cream was manufactured in Los Angeles, and two Romaine factotums sped it out across the desert in a refrigerated truck. They drove all night with it, modern Wells-Fargo lash-up-the-horses coachmen, and arrived in the morning.

The food manager at the Desert Inn, Dick Porcaro, had been alerted that some ice cream was coming in for Hughes and that it was supposed to be kept secret.

When the driver backed up the truck, Porcaro got two jolts. "I didn't know there was going to be *350 gallons* of ice cream," he recently recalled. "And the 'secret' ice cream was concealed under a bunch of blankets with HUGHES PRODUCTIONS printed on them."

Porcaro called Margulis on the phone. "Where in the hell are we supposed to store 350 gallons of ice cream?" he asked.

"Put it in the kitchen refrigerator room," Margulis said. All the restaurant storage of frozen food had to be rearranged, but the great stockpile of banana-nut ice cream was finally tucked away.

"We still had a few scoops of the old banana-nut left when the new banana-nut arrived," Margulis says. "Now we were all set with ice cream for the rest of Hughes's lifetime."

When the ice cream was served to Hughes the next day, he ate it and declared, "That's great ice cream, but it's time for a change. From now on, I want French vanilla."

It took the Desert Inn almost a year to get rid of the stockpile of ice cream. Mell Stewart, who had created the storage problem, helped solve it. "I'd go up to people I knew only casually and ask them if they liked Baskin-Robbins banana-nut ice cream. If they said yes, I'd give them a couple of gallons. I became known as a man who was very generous with ice cream."

Hughes attached his secrecy fetish to everything connected with him. In his multimillion-dollar business transactions, this made sense. The price of a coveted parcel of land would skyrocket if it became known that he wanted it.

But he was equally secretive about little things, such as his hospital alcohol and his apple strudel.

He heard that the Sands, another resort he had bought, had a superior bakery. He tried a number of its desserts and zeroed in on the Sands apple strudel.

The Sands is a few block down the Strip from the Desert Inn. This created a security problem. Margulis offered to go down and fetch the strudel, but Hughes overruled this. "Don't let Gordon get the apple strudel," he instructed the aides. "People know

Gordon works for me and they'll put two and two together. Send the guard for the strudel."

Whenever Hughes wanted apple strudel, the guard would be relieved and dispatched to the Sands for it. One night there was no extra guard available. The aides were faced with a dilemma. They could leave Hughes unguarded (except for the special elevator lock and two intervening locked doors) or risk blowing Hughes's apple strudel cover. They resolved this dilemma by pressing the chief of the Desert Inn security force into service as strudel courier.

"You had to live in that world quite a while before you believed it," said Pat Margulis, Gordon's slim, blonde wife. Her words echoed those of Bob Maheu. When he took the witness stand in 1974 in his defamation suit against his former employer, reporters asked how long he expected to testify. "It is going to take a while," he said, "to explain the unbelievable world of Howard Hughes."

Some of Hughes's problems were readily solved. One of the Las Vegas legends, that he bought KLAS-TV (Channel 8) television station because he liked to watch late movies, is true.

"A Hughes aide called me and said Hughes wanted the station to run movies all night," says Hank Greenspun, who owned the station. "I said it wasn't economically feasible. He still wanted all-night movies, so I suggested that he buy the station. He bought the station, and they started running all-night movies."

Hughes spent an enormous amount of time watching movies, both on TV and with his own screen and projector. After his move to Nassau, he had to depend upon his own projector because the TV reception was bad.

"He liked any kind of plane picture except *Waldo Pepper* with Robert Redford. He didn't like the comedy sequences," says Margulis. "He thought *The Blue Max* with George Peppard was great.

"He bought prints of all the James Bond pictures, but he liked only the ones with Sean Connery. His other favorites were *The Sting, Butch Cassidy and the Sundance Kid, The Clansman* and *The High Commissioner*.

"He detested *Myra Breckenridge*. He ran it once and said, 'When they're making so many movies, why can't they make pictures that I enjoy?' "

Ice Station Zebra will probably remain indelibly imprinted on the minds of his entourage for the rest of their lives. After Hughes's death, Margulis was talking to some friends, and the television was on in the adjoining room. There came drifting in a few bars of theme music, heavy with kettledrums.

"They're running *Ice Station Zebra*," said Margulis. "Switch the channel!"

Margulis says that Hughes was fascinated with the submarine technology in *Zebra*, which deals with a journey by a nuclear sub under the Arctic icecap on a secret mission against the Russians. "There was one thing that bothered him. He kept complaining that they had put the nuclear power plant in the wrong place."

In his latter days the movies he liked dealt with incredible feats of personal daring, great coups of deception, and intrigue, gadgetry, and technology. Few of them had any strong romantic theme or love interest. When they did, Hughes would tell his aide to "skip those mushy parts."

In the movies he had made when young, there were beautiful women who were wooed and won or lost. *Ice Station Zebra* had no women in it at all. Neither did Hughes's last ten years.

He made one final chess move, however, calculated to fetch Jean Peters out to Las Vegas. One of their problems, some of the aides whispered behind their hands, was that he had kept himself isolated during the last day at Bel Air, and had required her to sit across the room from him during her brief visit in Boston. He decided that he would obtain a luxurious home for her in Las Vegas. Why he wanted her there, if his phobias would not let him go near her, is puzzling. But what he wanted, the organization jumped to obtain.

His agents scouted up an impressive residence near the swank Rancho Circle area. This is a wooded enclave, fed by artesian wells, that resembles a pleasant oasis in the generally parched Las Vegas landscape. The homes there, built for the original casino nabobs and entertainers (residents include Johnny Carson, comedian Buddy Hackett, Phyllis Maguire), can look anything in Bel Air squarely in the picture window.

The home chosen for Jean Peters, without her knowledge, was the residence of Major Riddle, owner of the Dunes hotel. It is a huge, one-story natural stone house at 2122 Edgewood Avenue on an impressive plot of land. It contains over 9,000 square feet of living space, including a 2,400-square-foot master bedroom area.

It had one drawback. Major Riddle wanted to sell it furnished, and Hughes wanted to lease it furnished. Riddle wouldn't yield, but Hughes prevailed. The head of a Las Vegas bank, where considerable Hughes funds were deposited, bought the house from Riddle for a reported $600,000, and then leased it to the Hughes organization.

Riddle was asked to evacuate the house at once and cleared out within forty-eight hours. Jean never set foot in it. It stood empty for years and was finally sold to a wealthy automobile dealer.

In 1970 the Hugheses ended the pretense of a functioning marriage, and Jean shortly after married Stanley Hough, a movie producer nearer her own age. Hughes had Maheu announce the end of the marriage. The announcement was the first verification by Hughes that there *had* been a marriage. There were rumors that he settled several millions on her, but these proved false. Hughes made an arrangement to pay her $70,000 a year for twenty years, the amount to be adjusted annually, using the federal consumer price index, to offset inflation. In return, Jean waived all claims against his estate.

The settlement did not contain the usual Hughes severance prohibition against Jean talking or writing about her life with Hughes. It was not necessary. She has consistently rebuffed offers for her memoirs. She told friends and several writers, "I will never talk about my life with Howard."

She was one of the few persons who said "No" to him without incurring his wrath. "He liked Jean," says Stewart, "and to the end he never said an ill word about her. He always said what a fine person she was, and he remained interested in her welfare."

"I didn't mean much happiness to her," he told Stewart in his last year. "Being tied down to a son of a bitch like me wasn't much of a life for her."

[ ]

Sometimes he would sit for hours, silent and brooding, in his little Desert Inn bedroom. He would gather the long hair streaming down his back, pull it up over the top of his head, then let it fall, gather it up, let it fall.

Then he would stir himself, pick up the telephone and dictate a list of new projects for Maheu. After the first great flush of purchases, the projects tended to drift off and go nowhere. He announced plans to build a 4,000-room addition to the Sands. He wrote his own press release on the great Sands addition, which would have been the largest hotel ever built anywhere.

Hughes promised "the most complete vacation and pleasure complex anywhere in the world—a complete city within itself—shops open twenty-four hours a day, one entire floor devoted to family recreation, the largest bowling alley and billiard and pool facility in the world, an ice skating rink, rooms for chess and bridge, Skee-Ball, table tennis and a theater for first-run unreleased motion pictures." It would have indoor and night golf on a miniature electronics course "designed that shots will feel just like shots outdoors and the spin of the ball . . . is even measured electronically and indicated to the players."

The new Sands would be "so carefully planned

and magnificently designed that any guest will have to make a supreme effort to be bored."

This great pleasure dome proved pure fantasy, intended to scare off any further incursions into Las Vegas by other resort entrepreneurs. Not a spadeful of earth was ever turned for construction.

He projected a new airport for the supersonic age and forgot about it, and a mammoth race track that never got beyond a vague concept, and he dickered for four casinos that he never bought. Or else he engaged in fantasy, like buying a huge fleet of superplanes. He wrote in one memo: ". . . the contract I just signed is an agreement with the Lockheed Aircraft Corp. for substantially more than one billion dollars, in purchase of the very latest (far more than anything flying) design of Jumbo-Jet. There is nothing like this airplane in process of design or construction anywhere in the world. Needless to say, I intend to get back in the air-carrier business . . . This also is known to nobody, and I must ask your all-out pledge of secrecy."

In this memo about a contract he hadn't signed, for planes he never bought, he wrote: "I just tore off the rest of the last page, because I stated the exact amount and the number of aircraft involved and, upon hindsight, I decided these figures should not be floating around, even in a sealed envelope."

He was now cloaking in secrecy things that hadn't happened.

Other times, after twisting his hair and letting it fall for hours, he would pick up the phone and tell Maheu:

"Bob, I'm lonesome."

[ ]

One day old white-haired Noah Dietrich, now far up in his seventies, came out to Las Vegas. Maheu heard he was in town and had lunch with him. It was a meeting of the smallest club in the world—the only two men who had served as the billionaire's prime minister. The younger wanted advice from the older.

Maheu was having money problems, just as Dietrich had had money problems, and for the same reason. To represent Hughes to the world effectively, one had to live high, belong to expensive clubs, entertain, stay in suites at the Madison in Washington, the Regency or Carlyle in New York, the Bel Air when in Los Angeles. The $520,000 a year Maheu received was not a real $520,000 a year. The tax bite was enormous, and what was left melted swiftly away playing Maheu-Hughes in the proper style.

Dietrich was sympathetic; he had run himself out in the same 24-karat rat maze.

"I have one piece of advice for you," Dietrich said. "Whatever you get from Hughes, get it now and get it in writing. His word isn't worth what lands on the bottom of a birdcage."

Maheu had an additional concern. "I became aware in 1968," he says, "that some of the Hughes people were pumping in false information to Hughes clearly intended to undermine me. Hughes told me about some of the incidents himself.

" 'This is the kind of cleavage they are trying to create between us,' " Maheu quotes Hughes. " 'We have to guard against it.'

"So I sent him a message," Maheu says. "I told

him that I could handle these ploys as long as we were in communication. But I asked him what would happen to me if something happened to him."

In due course, Maheu got something in writing. It was a handwritten memo, and it read:

I have your message. I do not feel your apprehension is the least bit unjustified. If I give you my word to find a solution promptly, such as a voting trust for my Hughes Tool Company stock, and if I put the formalities into a state of effectiveness for your scrutiny without any unreasonable delay, will you consider it done as of now, so your mind will not be filled with these thoughts in the near future? I will assume an affirmative answer and proceed accordingly.

Maheu was euphoric. He put the memo in a safety-deposit box and went back to playing Maheu-Hughes with renewed vigor.

A voting trust for my Hughes Tool Company stock. That was the key to the golden cornucopia of the whole Hughes empire. Hughes had never let out a single share of Toolco stock to anyone. If he entrusted *all* of it to Maheu . . .

Visions of sugar plums clouded his vision. By his own admission, Maheu was no cold-eyed businessman. When documents were involved, he called in lawyers. But he couldn't show this document to a lawyer; it was a reassurance from the heart of Hughes to a troubled associate.

The memo, of course, was worth the one sheet of legal-sized yellow notebook paper it was written on. Those two little "if's," so swiftly slid over, were much larger and substantive than the "promptly," the "voting trust," the "state of effectiveness," the "without any unreasonable delay," "consider it done as of now," and "proceed accordingly."

But when the time came, Hughes executed a voting proxy, a real one without any "if's" in it.

It was not made out in favor of Bob Maheu. It named Bill Gay, Chester Davis, and Raymond Holliday. Then they used it, with Hughes's blessing, to push Maheu off the mountain top.

[6]
TOPPLING MAHEU

"**H**e loved to manipulate people," says Gordon Margulis. "He would praise one aide highly, to get him to do something difficult, unreasonable, or unpleasant. Then he would tell the next aide, 'I'm glad you're on duty. That fellow can't do a fucking thing right.' He was a master at playing one person off against another."

In 1968 Hughes began playing Maheu against Chester Davis, and vice versa. Davis had borne the brunt of the TWA legal battle from the beginning. When Hughes had sought legal counsel at the outset of the court fight, back in the early 1960's, his agents could not find a top-flight New York firm that could handle his case. Most of the big firms represented the financial institutions lined up against Hughes. They could not take on Hughes as a client because of conflict of interest.

Chester Davis was then with the prestigious law firm of Simpson, Thacher & Bartlett, old-line and blue-blood. He had been there for years and had the reputation of being a superb trial lawyer, a hard-driving, go-for-the-jugular fighter. Other members of the firm admired his competence but occasionally lifted an Ivy League eyebrow at his ambition and abrasive manners.

Even his closest friends at Simpson, Thacher didn't know his true origin. He was believed to have come from an "old money" New Jersey family, although Martingdale's legal directory bore the terse notation "b. Rome, Italy, Oct. 14, 1910." Those who knew of his birth in Rome thought that his father, Chester Davis, Sr., and mother had happened to be in Italy at the time.

Davis was actually Caesar Simon, the son of an Italian mother and Algerian father. His father had died when he was young, and his mother immigrated to the United States in 1922 when Caesar was twelve years old. She had married the senior Davis, and on November 15, 1935, in the U.S. District Court at Newark, New Jersey, Caesar Simon renounced his allegiance to King Victor Emmanuel III, became a U.S. citizen, and changed his name to Chester C. Davis, Jr. He attended good schools and got his law degree from Harvard, but his veins flowed with the hot blood of his Mediterranean origin.

After he was approached on the Hughes TWA case, Davis discovered that Simpson, Thacher & Bartlett also had a conflict of interest in the case. But Davis offered a solution. He would resign from Simpson, Thacher, set up his own virginal law firm, with no ties to anyone, and take on the Hughes organization as his client. He quit Simpson, Thacher and moved into quarters in the Wall Street area. When the huge fees from Hughes flowed in, he moved again to a handsome set of rooms at One State Street Plaza. From his office he could look out and down on the Statue of Liberty, past whose lifted lamp he had sailed as a boy of twelve.

At the outset the Hughes interests were his firm's lone client, and they remain the firm's chief client. Representing Hughes posed massive difficulties. Technically, Davis represented Hughes Tool Co., not the billionaire, but the details of the TWA transactions were largely locked up in Hughes's head. Chester Davis not only had a client who wouldn't see him, he had one that a herd of wild horses couldn't drag into court or a law office. Nevertheless, he fought brilliantly, doggedly (and profitably) for years. He also fought unsuccessfully, all the way up to the U.S. Supreme Court.

In September, 1968, the special master in the TWA case, former Attorney General Herbert Brownell, came out with a damage recommendation of $131,611,435.95 against Hughes Tool Co.—which meant Howard Hughes. It was a harsh setback for Davis and a worse one for Hughes, who had been assured that the damages at most would not run over $5 million.

On December 23, 1969—the day before Hughes's birthday—the judge in the TWA case, Judge Charles Metzner, approved Brownell's findings and upped the penalty—for costs and attorney fees—to a staggering $145,448,141.07.

In his cramped little bedroom, Hughes lay on his reclining chair and inveighed against an unjust world. "A fine goddamned birthday present *that* is," he told his aides.

When, with the Brownell finding, the case began to run against Davis, Hughes had shifted the overall responsibility for it to Maheu. Aware of the awesome stakes involved, Maheu had told Hughes that he wanted his authority in writing from the directors of Hughes Tool Co.

"Well, pick up the telephone and tell them what you want," Hughes said.

But Maheu demurred. "On something of this magnitude, I think their instructions should come from you, not me," he told the billionaire. Shortly Maheu had received his authorization from the Toolco board.

When Judge Metzner put the court's stamp of approval on the huge judgment, Hughes sent Maheu another memo. It reiterated and broadened his authority and contained a subtle hint.

"Bob, please understand one thing which I do not think you understood heretofore: You have the ball on the TWA situation." He said he didn't want to be bothered until Maheu had a final solution.

"I say again," he wrote, "you have full authority to do what you deem best in this entire matter . . . Also the decision of *what to do about legal representation is up to you.* [Italics added.]

"If I am to hold you responsible for the overall outcome of this litigation, I must give you the *complete authority to decide which law firm you want to handle each phase of it.*" [Italics added.]

Maheu consulted three well-known law firms, including that headed by Clark Clifford, former U.S. Defense Secretary. He then mapped a strategy. As summarized in Tinnin's case study of the TWA litigation:

> In essence, they told him that a whole new strategy had to be devised for the appeal. That strategy should rest on the assertion that Howard Hughes had been insufficiently represented in the lower court . . . But the problem was that such an approach would involve the repudiation of the conduct of case up until then. That meant a scapegoat would have to be found. And who would that sacrificial billy be? It could only be Chester Davis. According to some of the advice, the name of Chester Davis should not even appear on Toolco's brief . . .

This posed a ticklish problem to Maheu. He knew that Chester Davis was an unlikely man to play sacrificial lamb; when crossed, he was more the enraged bull. His firm had most of its legal eggs in the Hughes basket, and Davis would not react kindly to someone stomping on it. Besides, Maheu and Davis had a friendly relationship going back eight or nine years, to the heady days when Maheu was shunting the TWA Hughes-hunters down blind alleys after false Hugheses, and Davis was charting his first legal moves. They had dined together, ridden executive jets together, drunk together, and coordinated their anti-TWA chess moves together. Each was also aware that they were essentially outsiders in the

Hughes world, resented by Romaine and Houston veterans whose tenure was longer.

Maheu tried to soften the blow to Davis's pride and minimize the threat to his pocketbook. He assured him that he would continue as chief counsel for the Hughes interests. But in the TWA case, someone else would move up front.

To make certain that Hughes understood that he was not starting a vendetta against Davis, Maheu says, he sent a memo summarizing the legal advice he had received up to the penthouse.

"I heard later from three sources," he says, "that it never reached Howard Hughes."

Napoleon complained that in the recesses of his palace an emperor is dependent upon news brought to him by his ministers. In his little bedroom Hughes was even more isolated. By his own decision, he had barred his prime minister, his chief counsel and his other top executives from his presence. Hughes was dependent upon information funneled to him by the senior aides, the ex-potato-chip salesman and former chauffeurs loyal to Bill Gay. They controlled the telephone switchboard, hand-carried the memos back and forth.

Maheu held the reins of power, but Bill Gay's appointees held the lines of communication.

"I suggested a number of times that Hughes and I have face-to-face meetings," Maheu says. "He always put me off. He said we'd do this eventually, but eventually never came."

Looking back on the palace struggle that he lost, Maheu says, "With the benefit of hindsight, I can see things I missed at the time. Put them together, and they make a fascinating jigsaw picture."

One day in 1969, shortly after Maheu got authority over the TWA case, one of the senior aides sought him out. He told Maheu, "Mr. Hughes asked me to tell you he wants all his memos back. I'm to collect them and take them up to the penthouse. He said he wants to go over them to review his projects, what has been accomplished and what still needs to be done."

Maheu gathered them up and gave him three hundred or more. Several of the more sensitive ones were sequestered at the Desert Inn in a safety-deposit box. There was only one key. His son and assistant, Peter, had the key, and Peter was out of town.

"The aide was so upset that I called a man and had the safety box burned open so we could get the contents," Maheu says. The aide hurried off with them, and with them went the written record of what Hughes had instructed Maheu to do.

"Once I was playing tennis with Bill Gay on one of his rare trips to Las Vegas," Maheu says. "One of the senior aides came down with a manila envelope. I got called away from the court for a telephone call. It took only a minute or so, and when I came back I saw Gay reading a number of my memos to Hughes. I didn't let on that I'd seen anything. At the time I dismissed it as mere nosiness."

Next Maheu got new instructions from Hughes. "I've decided not to ask you to write me any more messages in longhand and sealed envelopes," the note said. "I know this is time consuming for you, and *my men think I don't trust them.* So, in the future, except

159

in rare instances, I prefer you dictate your reply to my messages via telephone and *whichever one of my men happens to be on duty.*" (Italics added.)

From then on, instead of going sealed directly to Hughes, Maheu's memos, suggestions, strategies, and plans went through the senior aides.

His only direct line of communication was now a phone call from Hughes. Hughes could call Maheu, but Maheu couldn't call Hughes. When he would call the penthouse, frequently the aides would tell him Hughes was sleeping, or not feeling well, or busy on another matter.

Then the calls from Hughes dwindled and finally stopped altogether. They stopped at a critical time—when Maheu had to make the decision about converting Chester Davis from a long-time friend into a "sacrificial billy."

Just when Maheu needed his support most, Hughes fell silent. From the penthouse came word from one of the senior aides that Hughes was not well and would be out of touch for a while. "He told me to carry on per existing directives," Maheu says. "This had happened before and didn't alarm me."

Maheu broke the bad news to Chester Davis, that someone else would move center stage on the TWA case. He got back a blistering message, telling him to quit tampering with Hughes's legal matters. The schism was swift, brutal, predictable.

Relying on Hughes's memo, giving him "full authority" over the TWA case and choice of a law firm, Maheu fired back a harsh reply via teletype.

"To date you have lost this case at every level with catastrophically adverse financial and other injury to the defendant . . . I have no confidence, in view of your unfortunate record thus far, that your presence will contribute to a successful appeal . . . the judgment now stands at a staggering figure. I deeply resent your presumptuous request that I 'cease interfering with counsel in charge of and responsible for the case.' There has been no intereference on my part other than taking steps to accord other counsel an opportunity to salvage a case which you have tragically lost."

While Maheu was battling with Davis, Hughes was secretly getting ready to abandon Las Vegas. The flight had been in the back of his mind for a year and a half, but he had told no one.

Gordon Margulis knew that Hughes had long had something in the works, but he didn't know what.

"I was told in 1969 to pack a bag and be ready to move out on a minute's notice. I packed the bag and kept it ready in my Desert Inn room. It was packed and waiting for 18 bloody months."

[ ]

By 1970 Hughes had lost his wife, lost the penultimate TWA court case, and now he was losing interest in Las Vegas as his baronial fiefdom. In his fifteen-by-seventeen bedroom, his word was law. But outside it, people didn't always respond properly.

Hughes was the most powerful man in Nevada. He had monitored the gambling statistics weekly, yearning to overtake and pass his two chief rivals, Dell Webb and William Harrah, with the most crap games, most slot machines, most blackjack tables, and highest percent of statewide play. With his last acquisition, Harold's Club in Reno, he finally became Nevada's No. 1 gambling boss. Politicians and state officials fawned on him. Vice-President Spiro Agnew came out from Washington to enjoy his absentee hospitality on a yacht cruise to Catalina. President Richard Nixon offered to send Henry Kissinger to Las Vegas to negotiate with him toward a détente over the AEC test-bomb issue.

But all this wasn't enough. He poured out his discontent in the summer of 1970 in a long telephone conversation with Maheu. The conversation was tape-recorded. It has a fascinating history. It was subpoenaed from Maheu's son, Peter, by the Hughes attorneys in Maheu's 1974 defamation suit against Hughes, and is one of the few firsthand accounts of how Hughes viewed his own world. Given his penchant for secrecy, it is ironic that this intimate Hughes discourse became accessible through the efforts of his own lawyers. The tape recording was never used at the trial, which made its filing as a defense exhibit all the more baffling.

With seven casinos, huge sections of the remaining available land on the Las Vegas Strip, an airport, a 548-acre ranch purchased from the widow of the German armament king, Alfred Krupp, his own television station, a 30,000-acre swatch of undeveloped land adjoining Las Vegas, and the state administration in his pocket, Hughes complained that he wanted more "freedom." The trouble with Nevada, he said, was that there were too many people who had to be dealt with.

"It just seems as if we were like somebody trying to move ahead with a mass of seaweed and other entanglements wrapped around him and holding him back, you know?" said the plaintive Hughes. "I don't pick up the paper one single day that I don't read about various conflicts in which we have a definite stake, a definite reason to be concerned, a definite reason to worry about the outcome. Every single one of these goddamn things requires attention. Every one could be a hazard to us. Everybody who gets a permit for a well around here and taps the water table is in effect a neighbor whose activities and aims have to be considered along with ours . . . So it means that every single move we make here has to be with due consideration of its effects on everyone else around here.

"I just wish we could find some place where we could start out with a clean sheet of paper and build a community that would be exactly the way we think it ought to be."

He said he had thought of getting a tract of land somewhere else in Nevada and trying to build the kind of city he had in mind, "where maybe we could have more freedom than we have here. But I don't think that would be a hell of a lot different . . . It would still be a part of Nevada no matter how you stack it up. I'm looking for a set-up where we'd have a little more freedom."

He had his eye on the Bahamas, he told Maheu. But Maheu had commissioned a political-economic survey of the Bahamas for him. The report, in deference to Hughes's love of secrecy, was given a private code name, "Downhill Racer." It warned Hughes that the government there was unstable. The natives, said Maheu, were getting restless. Just a few days earlier, some of the blacks had been displeased with the service they got in a "Kentucky Colonel place" and "the next night blew up the goddamn place." He told Hughes that "the Bay Street boys"—the whites who then ran Nassau—"were really rough on the colored."

Hughes had difficulty comprehending this. "Well why in the hell? The Nassau crowd hasn't been mistreated. They've been riding in the carpet of luxury, haven't they? . . . I thought the colored people down there—all the hotel employees and all—seemed to thrive as far as I could make out . . . tips have been good and I always thought the colored people had it pretty good around Nassau."

He let his mind range over the map, trying to pick a place that would suit his wishes. He had been "led to believe that Puerto Rico would turn the place upside for us, but the geographical location is not much to my liking." The smaller islands and keys off Florida didn't have the kind of hotel "with a degree of comfort that I would want." Mexico was "even worse." Hawaii was all right "from a physical and geographical standpoint," but "we'd just be subject to all the same restraints and problems there that we would in Nevada."

He kept coming back to the Bahamas, which is where he wanted to go. Maheu's adverse report irritated him. In his mind he came up with a solution that only Howard Hughes could have conceived.

"If I were to make this move," he said, "I would expect you really to wrap that government up down there to a point where it would be—well—a captive entity in every way."

The phone call was one of the last Maheu received from Hughes. A month or so later, Nevada elected a new governor to replace Laxalt, who could not succeed himself. Hughes had decided that Laxalt's lieutenant governor, Howard Fike, was the proper fellow to follow in the steps of the cooperative Laxalt, and Hughes had generously supported the Republican candidate's campaign. The voters of Nevada instead elected an independent-minded Irish Democrat and ex-marine, Mike O'Callaghan. The intransigence of the citizenry confirmed Hughes's low opinion of Nevada; his path was now entangled with more seaweed in the form of a governor who owed him nothing.

At about the same time, he received a crueler blow. On the basis of information funneled into his isolated little bedroom, he became convinced that Bob Maheu had deceived him and was stealing huge sums of his money. His alter ego, the man he confided in, consulted as an equal, deferred to, and splendidly arrayed with the trappings and the authority to play Hughes to the world, had repaid him—Hughes was told—with betrayal.

Who played Iago to Hughes's Othello, who convinced him that Maheu was a thief, and what information they used, will probably never be known.

But two things are certain. Hughes believed the charges against Maheu. And it has since been determined, in the legal arena where truth is tested, that the charges were false.

Two years after Hughes fled Las Vegas, in his famous telephonic interview repudiating Clifford Irving's fake autobiography, a reporter asked why he had fired Maheu. Hughes blurted out in anger, "Because he was a no-good, dishonest son of a bitch who stole me blind." The NBC moderator for the interview, Roy Neal, tried to divert him to other subjects, but Hughes plunged on. He said that it seemed unlikely that such a thing could happen with modern accounting methods, "but the money is gone and he's got it."

In the ensuing defamation case filed by Maheu, a battery of Hughes attorneys stipulated that Hughes's words were libelous if untrue and pleaded truth as his lone defense. They commissioned the national private investigation agency Intertel to document Hughes's charge. Intertel conducted 525 separate investigations of Maheu, combed records, interrogated hundreds of his associates, friends, enemies. With all this massive research, Hughes's lawyers couldn't prove Hughes's charge. After a five-month trial, the jury unanimously ruled against Hughes and in favor of Maheu, and awarded him $2,800,000 in damages.

But in that bleak November in 1970, when he became poisoned against Maheu, Hughes faced an agonizing problem. In the old days he could have picked up the telephone, ordered Noah Dietrich, "Fire the son of a bitch!" and then vanished into absentia. He had always cringed away from confrontations; one of the rewards of great power is the delegation of unpleasant tasks to others.

He could fire Maheu himself. But he had been sicker in recent weeks than he had been in his whole stay in Las Vegas. Dr. Feikes had been spirited up to the penthouse again and found him in sad shape, suffering from pneumonia and nutritional anemia, and with a hemoglobin count of four rather than the normal fourteen or more. He administered a massive blood transfusion, and it was only now beginning to restore Hughes to what had become his normal state of fragile health.

He had neither the strength or spirit or desire to take on Bob Maheu. In the good days of the past, when Maheu was foiling his enemies, booby-trapping them, running them into ditches, Hughes had often told him admiringly, "Bob, I wouldn't want you for an enemy." There had been the time, shortly after their arrival in Las Vegas, when a junkie-burglar had broken into Maheu's house at midnight. The intruder fled when Maheu switched on the lights, but Maheu took after him, unarmed, and captured him single-handed in a wild pursuit around the Desert Inn pool.

Since Hughes couldn't bring himself to fell Maheu, he had to create an executioner. This required an extraordinary delegation of Hughes's power.

He sent three men to do the job he himself couldn't face. On November 14 he executed a proxy authorizing Chester Davis, Bill Gay, and Raymond Holliday to act "in my name and stead" and "exercise all rights I may have as a stockholder." The sweeping proxy had a canny reservation: the trio was forbidden to sell, dispose of, or transfer any of his holdings.

The document was drafted in the New York law office of Chester Davis and sped by wire to the Desert Inn penthouse. Later there was testimony that the proxy had been discussed for three months by Bill Gay, Chester Davis, and the Palace Guards.

Senior aide Howard Eckersley took the proxy into the cramped little bedroom, trailed by pudgy Levar

Myler. Hughes was seated in his old Barcalounge, wan and silent. Eckersley handed the proxy to Hughes. It was unusual for *two* aides to invade his darkened lair at one time, and Hughes looked up from the document, gestured to his faithful Myler, and asked plaintively:

"What's *he* doing here?"

"I'm the notary," Eckersley explained, "and Levar is here to sign as a witness. There has to be a witness."

Hughes nodded, put the proxy on his legal pad and tried to sign it. The pad was an unsatisfactory desk.

"More pads," Hughes ordered.

The aides gathered a stack and Hughes affixed his signature. Then Hughes handed the document to Myler, told him to put it in a safety-deposit box, and hold it for further instructions.

Myler scurried off and put it in his own strong box at his bank. He then made a single telephone call. The phone call was to Bill Gay, and later under oath Myler testified that Gay was the only person in the Hughes empire to whom he disclosed that the proxy was signed, notarized, and ready to be used.

The corporate guillotine was complete and the blade in place. It needed only the nod from Hughes, and Maheu's head would roll.

But first there was a series of projects assigned to the Hughes Secrecy Machine. Hughes not only did not want to fire Maheu himself, he wanted to be far from the scene when the deed was done. And he was in poor shape to be moved anywhere.

He had decided to go to the Bahamas, despite

Maheu's warning that black unrest and discontent there made it a perilous haven. It was, indeed, an odd place for a billionaire with the archaic notion that the natives ought to be content and happy with tourists' tips. Given Hughes's willfulness and his resentment toward Maheu, he may have picked Nassau just to prove Maheu wrong. He would not only use a new enemy of Maheu, Chester Davis, and an old one, Bill Gay, to depose him, but he would issue the "fire him" order from the very place Maheu had told him to shun.

He went to Nassau, and Maheu proved to be right in his appraisal. Instead of humbling Maheu, Hughes found himself humiliated beyond any outrage he had ever experienced in his life. Rather than wrapping up the government there as "a captive entity in every way," he barely escaped captivity himself.

[7]
FLIGHT
FROM THE D.I.

Operation Exit Las Vegas went off superbly. The aides whisked Hughes out of the Desert Inn unseen and installed him in another little blacked-out bedroom in the Bahamas before anyone—including his own guards—knew he had left Las Vegas.

So well did the Secrecy Machine function that Hughes's flight from the Desert Inn inspired a whole new collection of myths. It became a kind of *Rashomon* in which each version was colored by the wishful thoughts, prejudices, or fantasies of those telling it.

Bob Maheu believed Hughes had been snatched away in a forcible palace coup. When he learned that Hughes was in the Britannia Beach Hotel on Paradise Island off Nassau, he sent a team of private investigators to determine whether Hughes was being held against his will. They even had a boat ready to "rescue" the billionaire if it turned out that he was a captive. Hughes's security agents discovered Maheu's men and had them evicted from the island.

Hank Greenspun, who first broke the story of Hughes's disappearance in the Las Vegas *Sun*, proclaimed that Hughes had been removed while inoperative and in a coma.

One "eyewitness" came forward and declared he had seen Hughes being hustled across the Desert Inn parking lot, crying, "Someone call Bob Maheu or Pat Hyland!"

A thin, tense woman, who wore dark sunglasses and refused to give her name, later buttonholed newsmen with "the true story of Hughes's disappearance from Las Vegas." She said the Mafia had "nicked his heart muscle" from afar with a laser beam, inducing an "artificial heart attack." The Mafioso had then taken him off to captivity to gain control of his gambling empire.

Time magazine gave a detailed account that brought smiles to those who engineered Hughes's removal. "A few minutes before ten o'clock on Thanksgiving eve," said *Time*, "Howard Hughes pulled an old sweater over the white shirt that he wore open at the neck, donned a fedora and walked to the rear of the penthouse atop the Desert Inn . . . Hughes eased his tall, thin frame through a long-unused fire door and walked the nine stories down an interior fire escape to the hotel parking lot."

Plans for the departure were a tightly kept secret until the evening before the flight.

Margulis sensed something was going on several

days before the word was passed. "There was an air of tension and a heavy flow of phone calls in and out of The Office. Before the departure, some of the aides began quietly removing boxes and equipment.

"The day before Thanksgiving, John Holmes passed the word to a selected few. 'We're moving out tonight,' Holmes said. 'Tell no one, and that means *no one*.' He did not tell me where they were taking Hughes."

Four of the five senior aides—Holmes, Eckersley, Myler, Francom—were in on the project. So were Margulis, Mell Stewart, Margulis's assistant, Carl Romm, and one physician, Dr. Norman Crane. Jack Real procured the plane, a Lockheed Jet Star. It was put in place at Nellis Air Force Base some thirteen miles northeast of Las Vegas. It had a private pilot and copilot from outside the Hughes organization. They were not told who was to be aboard.

A small group of limousines from Romaine were parked in the lot behind the Desert Inn as decoys.

News of the impending abandonment of the penthouse was withheld from the fifth senior aide, Roy Crawford, although he was one of the most trusted aides and had served in the inner circle ever since Hughes had vanished from public view years before. But Crawford had been the chief courier between Hughes and Maheu and had developed a close relationship—at Hughes's instructions—with *Sun* publisher Hank Greenspun. Maheu also had cultivated Greenspun at Hughes's instructions. Hughes had purchased Greenspun's TV station and his Paradise Valley golf course, and had loaned Greenspun $3 million at only 4 percent interest. "I guess he thought he was buying me along with the properties," said Greenspun. "He learned otherwise."

Maheu had dealt with Greenspun on these transactions but had acted as Hughes's agent and kept Hughes advised of the details in a series of memos. Each time, when the transaction was reduced to writing and formalized, Hughes approved it and the closeout was handled by Hughes's own lawyers.

One of the drawbacks of the tightly compartmentalized Hughes Secrecy Machine was that one part didn't know what another part was doing. The division assigned to remove Hughes from the Desert Inn knew only that Maheu had suddenly become "the enemy." Crawford had been too close to both Maheu and Greenspun and was now "tainted." So he was blocked off from knowledge that Hughes was fleeing Las Vegas.

On the evening of the flight Crawford was off duty. The aides used Margulis to keep Crawford in the dark about the impending move.

Crawford and some friends were having dinner that evening at the Desert Inn's Monte Carlo Room. Margulis was aware of this. "What do you want to do about Roy?" Margulis asked one of the aides.

"He's attending a wedding party," the aide said. "He's been working hard lately and we're not going to bother him and spoil his evening. If you happen to see him, *don't tell him a word*. Let him enjoy his party."

"I believed what I was told," says Margulis. "I didn't know Crawford was being cut out of the inner circle until much later. A day or so after Hughes left,

I bumped into Roy and asked him how he had enjoyed the wedding party.

"Roy looked at me like I'd gone balmy. *'What wedding party?'* he asked. I mumbled something and walked away."

Crawford, of course, was kept on the payroll. He was a walking repository for many of Hughes's secrets. He was transferred back to the Gay-Henley base in California. He is still a Summa employee.

Late that night the mission was ready to go into operation. Margulis was summoned to the ninth floor and passed through the locked door behind the guard, and through the locked door of The Office.

The door to Hughes's bedroom opened and the billionaire was brought out on a stretcher. His gray hair, a foot and a half long, was incongruously topped by a snap-brim brown Stetson, the kind that had been his trademark back in the 1930's when he was breaking world records as a pilot. (Months earlier Mell Stewart had scoured Las Vegas men's shops to find the Stetson. Hughes had insisted that the proper out-of-date hat be found for him.) His eyes were sunken, with dark circles under them, and his weight was down around 115 pounds. He was clad in a pair of blue pajamas, and from what Gordon could see, his legs and lower arms were almost bone thin.

He was lying face up on the stretcher with a pillow covered by a plastic bag under his head.

"He was in bad shape, but he was lucid and coherent," says Margulis. "He looked up at me and said, 'Hi, Gordon.'

"We picked him up. I took the front end of the

stretcher with Eckersley, Holmes, and Francom at the other end."

The penthouse floor has two interior fire escapes. One opens off the elevator landing where the guard was stationed. The other is at the far end of the corridor and exits on the Strip side of the Desert Inn. The departure was made by this path so that Hughes could not be seen by his own guard.

The silent group moved out of The Office, turned right and went down the fire escape. Margulis went first, holding the front of the stretcher high to keep it level. They descended carefully, a step at a time, for nine floors, like a solemn religious procession bearing aloft a sacred relic or ikon.

"It's pretty narrow in here," Hughes piped up during the descent. "I guess it's a good thing I've lost weight."

"Keep your arms at your side," Margulis cautioned him, "and we'll make it all right."

On the ground floor a lookout signaled all-clear, and the pace quickened. The stretcher was swiftly placed in a waiting, unmarked van. Eckersley, Holmes, and Francom piled in, and the van slid out onto the deserted Strip and headed for Nellis.

At Nellis the two pilots were ordered to walk off in the darkness and face away from the plane. The stretcher with Hughes was put aboard and the rest of the party followed. It consisted of Holmes, Eckersley, Myler, Francom, Carl Romm, and Dr. Norman Crane. With Hughes sequestered in the rear of the plane, the two pilots were allowed to board but were warned not to look back at any time during the flight.

Meanwhile, shortly before Hughes was taken from the Desert Inn, another small party had boarded the Romaine limousines at the rear of the hotel. They had moved out together; in plain sight of any onlookers, and sped off to McCarran Airport. This motorized red herring was intended to lure off any enemies, spies, or whatever, and take them down a blind alley. It proved unnecessary; the billionaire's flight from his lair went undetected.

After he had put Hughes in the van, Margulis and one of the functionaries went to a public phone at a hamburger stand about a mile away, waited a few minutes, and then made a phone call. "Everything OK?" the functionary asked. "They've taken off," he was told.

The phone call, by prearrangement, was made to the Romaine switchboard. The long-bypassed control center was now back in control. Maheu's communications were severed, the penthouse was no longer functional, and Bill Gay was back in the action.

On Thanksgiving Day, Margulis went through a charade to establish that Hughes, by then safely hidden 3,000 miles away, was still on the ninth floor of the Desert Inn. He went down to the Desert Inn kitchen in the morning and ordered a "special turkey dinner for the boss." The chefs spent most of the day preparing it. When it was ready, Margulis put it on a serving cart, wheeled it to the elevator, and took it up to the abandoned penthouse.

"Dinner for the boss," he told the guard, as he pushed the cart through the partition door. The dinner was consumed by two functionaries. The same day, Chuck Waldron came in and changed all the locks on the ninth floor to make certain the secret of Hughes's flight was preserved as long as possible.

While Margulis went through the motions of serving meals for the vanished Hughes, Stewart and three others—Eric Bundy, Norm Love, and Fred Jayka—cleaned up the billionaire's little bedroom.

"It was—well, pretty awful," says Stewart. "There hadn't been a maid in the room for four years, and it had never been vacuumed or dusted." The memory is plainly distasteful to Stewart and he is reluctant to talk about it.

Stewart's job was to dispose of Hughes's empty bottles of pain-killing drugs. They had been stacked on a wide shelf in the bedroom closet, and when Stewart opened the door he was astonished at the sight.

"There must have been a hundred of them," he says. "I didn't count them, but they were stacked on top of each other, and they almost filled the shelf space."

Stewart's first instructions were to put them in a gunnysack, smash them with a hammer, and bury the sack of broken bottles at some remote spot far out in the desert. Then his instructions were changed. He was told to pack the bottles in boxes and deliver them to the Romaine headquarters.

"I had my wife drive me from Las Vegas to Los Angeles," Stewart says. "I turned over the empty bottles to the Romaine staff. I don't know why they wanted them, and I didn't ask."

The three functionaries had to deal with an even darker Hughes secret. For years he had had the habit of urinating into a wide-mouthed Mason jar while reclining on his lounge chair. His kidneys were malfunctioning long before they failed in Acapulco and precipitated his death. Relieving himself took hours, and he was too weak to sit all that time in the bathroom. Instead of being emptied, the jars had been capped and stacked in a corner of his little bedroom. The employees had to get rid of a three-year supply of Hughes's urine and then wash and destroy the jars. One aide kept interrupting the job to go off into an adjoining bathroom and retch.

When they were finished, and Stewart had removed the empty drug bottles, the Desert Inn housekeeping crew came in for the final cleanup. They took the old draperies, and some of the sheets and towels, and burned them; the room had to deodorized.

A few of the house-cleaning staff whispered stories to their closest friends—with warnings never to speak a word about what they were told. They told others, with the same warning. Rumors spread that there was something dreadfully wrong with the billionaire who owned Desert Inn and much of Las Vegas.

But there was already such a confusion of myths about Hughes that many who heard this new story passed it off as another fabrication.

Maheu heard these rumors soon after he learned that Hughes had been taken out of the Desert Inn, but before he was told he was fired. He already knew there was something wrong with Hughes, but he didn't know the details. When Hughes had left Boston to come out to Las Vegas in 1966, Maheu knew that two aides had to stay behind and clean up his bedroom at the Copley-Plaza Hotel there. The new stories propelled him to the wrong conclusion.

He assumed that Hughes had totally ceased to function and that others were acting in his stead.

When he was told a week later that Hughes had fired him, Maheu didn't believe it. There was logic in his reasoning, and in his conclusion that someone other than Hughes had issued the order.

"The last time I had talked to him," Maheu says, "there was no inkling that I was out of favor. He had assured me repeatedly that I was to be with him the rest of his life, and warned me not to let the Romaine-Houston people drive a wedge between us. I had a half-dozen projects in the works for him.

"And finally, I had been hired by Hughes as his chief executive officer, and if I was to be fired, Hughes was the man to do it.

"All it would have taken was a single phone call from him. If he had telephoned me and said, 'Bob, you and I have come to the end of the road and I'm going to replace you,' I'd have said so-long and walked away. I couldn't believe that Hughes was unwilling to pick up the phone and give me that simple message."

Maheu said the same thing publicly. "If I've been fired," he told reporters, "I want to hear it from Howard Hughes." The phone call never came. Like old Noah Dietrich, Maheu never again heard from his ex-employer.

[8]
THE IRVING HOAX

At the Britannia Beach Hotel the security was cinched down even tighter than it had been at the Desert Inn. The Hughes party had only half of the top floor, so the Hughes half was sealed off from the rest of the floor with a special partition. There was now a double set of guards—one at the elevator to make certain you belonged on the floor, another beyond the locked partition to control traffic in and out of the Hughes party's suites. Beyond the inner guard was a *second* partition so that again—as at the Desert Inn—the guard couldn't observe what went on in the suite.

The inner guard had four closed-circuit TV screens by which he monitored the hall, the roof, the front of the hotel, and the back of it. Patrolling the roof was yet another guard with a huge German shepherd.

Dr. Chaffin and Mell Stewart used the move to

Nassau to get Hughes out of the lounge chair he had been living and sleeping in for four years. The pressure sores on his back were now so severe that the scapula bone on his shoulder was protruding and visible. Hughes agreed reluctantly to try sleeping in a bed and let Dr. Chaffin and Stewart sponge his bedsores and treat them with medication. The sores were so deep and of such long duration that they never healed completely.

Hughes was transferred to a motorized hospital bed that he could control himself. He could raise himself up into a sitting position or return to the horizontal by pushing buttons. The aides were not permitted merely to move the bed into his room and put Hughes into it. Hughes selected the exact position where he wanted the bed installed. It had to be precisely aligned the way he wanted it, with tape marks on the floor specifying where the legs of the bed were to be placed.

There were other routines to be followed which created logistic problems. The aides had to establish a dependable source for Poland water. Hughes was the original "Don't drink the water" American traveler. He didn't trust even the water supply in his native country. For more than twenty years he had drunk only bottled water and insisted that only bottled water be used in cooking his meals. It had to be Poland water, in quarts only, and bottled at the company's original plant in Maine. He liked it ice-cold, just short of freezing. He would not drink from a glass; he demanded a fresh Styrofoam plastic container that could be discarded after being used once. At intervals he would question the aides as to whether the water was *really* Poland bottled water; once he insisted upon being carried to the storage cabinet so that he could verify that the aides indeed had an adequate supply of the bottled water on hand.

For some reason he distrusted the pint-sized individual bottles of Poland water. The Las Vegas distributor once related that he was out of the quart bottles when the Hughes aides put in an order and he had filled it with pint bottles. The order had been returned, with stern instructions never to fill a Hughes order with pints. "I had to call all over Southern California to rustle up some quarts and have them shipped out to Las Vegas," the distributor said. "I never did figure out what this was all about, because it was the same water."

Hughes also refused to drink any Bahamian milk. Only Florida-bottled milk was acceptable. The aides, fortunately, located a Nassau market that handled milk out of Florida and thus were relieved of establishing a regular milk run to the mainland.

With their clean-up work concluded at the Desert Inn, the rest of the entourage joined the Hughes party at Paradise Island.

The group stayed at the Britannia Beach Hotel for fifteen months. The stay in the Bahamas started off badly and wound up in near disaster.

On December 4, 1970, two days after the Las Vegas *Sun* ran a story bannerlined HOWARD HUGHES MISSING, Hughes pushed the button and ordered the severance of Maheu. Levar Myler telephoned his wife in Las Vegas and told her to get the proxy out of their safety-deposit box and turn it over to Chester Davis.

Davis summoned a friend of Maheu's, the Washington lawyer Edward Morgan, to a brief meeting at the Century Plaza Hotel in Los Angeles. He informed Morgan that Maheu was off the payroll and that he had until sundown to resign or be fired.

Morgan flew back to Las Vegas with the ultimatum, but Davis didn't wait for an answer. He sped to Las Vegas by executive jet and took over the top floor of the Sands Hotel as a battle station. Having heard that Las Vegas was a hornet's nest of bugs and wiretaps, he addressed a fancied microphone in the ceiling of his Sands suite with a message for Maheu. "If you're up there, you son of a bitch," Davis called out, "you're going to jail!"

Maheu, instead, went to court. While he was vainly trying to get in touch with Hughes by telephone, he got word from the Hughes casinos that the Davis-Gay forces were moving strangers into the cashier cages to take over the money and records. The casino cages are the *sancta sanctorum* of the gambling houses. They are the repositories for the supply of casino chips, for all the lovely money the tourists are trying to win, and for all the "markers"—IOU's and checks—of those who have tried and failed. Nevada law forbids anyone to enter the cages except those specifically approved by the casino owners and certified by the state gambling authorities to be trustworthy fellows.

"All of a sudden there was this swarm of Mongolian monks from Mars invading the cages," Maheu said. "I checked with Tom Bell, Hughes's personal attorney. He warned me that the state could revoke the Hughes gambling licenses for this violation of the rules."

("That 'Mongolian monks from Mars' was a nice touch of exaggeration," a pro-Davis lawyer sniffed later. "Actually, they were Haskin-Sells auditors and security agents from Intertel.")

Whoever they were, their invasion of the cages was improper. A Las Vegas judge granted Maheu an injuction against the Davis-Gay forces, and the casino invaders retreated. The "shoot-out at the Hughes corral," as *Time* described it, was now on in earnest.

The Las Vegas battle fetched newsmen by the dozen, and by mid-December Hughes was front-page news across the country. The Hughes flight from the Desert Inn, so secretive, successful, and silent, erupted into a major media happening, with raucous charges and countercharges, shouts of triumph, and wailing from the wounded. If Hughes had planned his flight as a publicity stunt, he could not have attracted more attention to himself by walking out of the Desert Inn at high noon leading a brass band.

Maheu scored in the early rounds by challenging the authenticity of Hughes's signature on the proxy granting his powers to the Davis-Gay forces. The challenge was not wholly frivolous. Among the senior aides, Maheu knew, were several adept at signing Hughes's name, and at least one document in the TWA case bearing Hughes's signature had been declared a forgery.

The Davis-Gay forces countered by arranging for Hughes to telephone Governor Laxalt—at 4:30 A.M. Hughes time and 1:30 A.M. in Nevada. Hughes expressed his firm support for Davis and Gay. He explained that he was just taking "a little vacation" and promised the governor that he would return to Las Vegas to live out the rest of his life. He was to live more than five years without ever seeing Las Vegas again.

Hughes followed up the telephone call with a handwritten letter headed "Dear Chester and Bill." The letter expressed disappointment that they had not been able to depose Maheu quietly, and complained about the "very damaging publicity." It authorized the pair to take "whatever action is necessary" to "terminate all relationship with Maheu," and requested an "immediate accounting" of all funds under Maheu's control.

The court reversed itself and restrained Maheu from exercising any authority over the Hughes Nevada operation. The exuberant victors ordered Maheu to vacate his mansion and drafted plans to put the casino licenses in the names of the Gay-Davis group.

The Palace coup was over, Maheu was out, and Davis and Gay were in. Glasses were clinked in a triumphant celebration at the Sands Hotel. Chester Davis tossed off his Scotch and roared with laughter. Bill Gay sipped his drink and smiled.

But the trouble wasn't ended. It was just beginning.

[ ]

The Secrecy Machine had worked too well. By keeping Hughes totally invisible for almost ten years, the Machine had reduced him to an improbable wraith and stripped him of credibility. A judge might be satisfied that a 1:30 A.M. phone call and a letter established that Hughes was a living, breathing, functioning proprietor of seven casinos, but hardly anyone else was convinced.

Las Vegas, by its nature, is a nervous and suspicious town. Someone was always trying to slip his own dice into a crap game, or put in the fix with a blackjack dealer. There was an old saying that after a Las Vegan shakes hands with a stranger, he counts his fingers. And Hughes was not only a stranger, but the strangest who had ever hit town. Other casino owners strolled through the gambling rooms, patted the pit-men and box-men on their backs, bought drinks for the high rollers, laughed at their jokes. Hughes had more than 6,000 employes, and he had come into town unseen, purchased their places of employment, and vanished unseen without ever so much as waving a ghostly hand from his penthouse window. Now Bob Maheu had been beheaded by a piece of paper with Hughes's name on it, and the Davis-Gay forces were busy lopping off scores of others from the Hughes payroll. Who was safe, and why had their employer vanished?

At the height of the uproar the new governor, Mike O'Callaghan, took office in Carson City. His new gaming control agency refused to approve the Davis-Gay plan for reorganization of the Hughes casinos, or to grant Chester Davis a license to act for Hughes. The new chairman of the gaming board said he thought that Hughes ought to sit down with the board and go over its problems in person.

The Hughes attorneys produced another letter, purportedly from the billionaire, asserting that the Gay-Davis proposals had his approval. They offered to have Hughes telephone Governor O'Callaghan *in person* from the far-off Bahamas.

O'Callaghan declined to talk on the phone with an invisible man. "I refused to get involved with game-playing by telephone and letter," he said. "I don't know the authenticity of it, and I'm getting fed up with the intrigue that surrounds the entire matter.

"Everyone says Hughes is in excellent health. But they always add that if he saw one of our people it would be traumatic. What's so traumatic about seeing someone?" It was a cogent question, but no answer was forthcoming. That was the ultimate secret the aides were guarding, and they were not about to divulge it just because a governor was getting querulous.

The noisy dethroning of Maheu had some lamentable fallout, from Hughes's viewpoint. In the court struggle over the authenticity of the Davis-Gay proxy, Levar Myler had to take the witness stand in Las Vegas to attest to witnessing Hughes's signature. Under cross-examination, further details about the proxy—how it was prepared, transmitted, and hidden away—were elicited over constant objections from the Hughes attorneys. When the perspiring Myler finally stepped down from the stand, a stern order was issued from the Britannia Beach Hotel. The State of Nevada was henceforth off limits to all of Hughes's personal staff. Hughes didn't want any more of this testifying under oath about the way he conducted his affairs. He invoked the same rule he had followed so successfully himself —avoid the court's jurisdiction.

This imposed hardships on those of his staff whose

families lived in Las Vegas. They could now no longer go home during their off-duty periods.

"It was bad enough under normal conditions," said Pat Margulis, Gordon's wife. "All the women who were married to members of the Hughes staff had to get along with part-time husbands. Then when the aides were ordered to stay out of Nevada, we couldn't see our husbands at all.

"I wouldn't put up with that. I closed the house and moved to Southern California so Gordon could visit me and the baby whenever he got time off. Some of the other wives of the aides moved out of Nevada too, so they could see their husbands now and then.

"When it began to look as if they were settled down permanently in the Bahamas, I took our little son and moved down there. The Hughes aides didn't like this, but I said to myself the hell with them.

"The rents around Nassau were frightfully high, so all I could afford was a tiny little place. But at least we had some sort of life together.

"Unless you were in the insider group, they looked upon a man's family as some sort of nuisance. Mr. Gay maintained a full-time suite for himself and his friends at the Emerald Beach Hotel in Nassau. Mr. Davis kept a leased yacht there, with a captain and his wife to tend it. But for men like Gordon—well, you'd never call it a life of luxury."

[ ]

In the early summer of 1971 some of the aides embarked upon a business venture of their own. It was a bold decision on their part. Hughes didn't approve of his aides or executives diluting their time and attention with outside endeavors. Besides, he felt that business ventures by people close to him could be construed as *his* ventures, and he was adamant against any exploitation of his name.

But when his staff aide, Howard Eckersley, took a disastrous flier in the mining business, Eckersley didn't tell Hughes about it. So tightly did the senior aides control Hughes's information that the billionaire was kept in the dark about the mining scandal for more than a year.

The mining scandal illustrated graphically Hughes's isolation from the world after Las Vegas. The story of Eckersley's fiasco was widely reported in the Las Vegas *Sun*, which first broke the story, in the Los Angeles *Times*, *The New York Times*, *The Wall Street Journal*, *Playboy* magazine, and the Canadian press, and was the subject of a one-hour documentary on the Canadian Broadcasting Network. Hughes's executives in Houston and Encino knew about it. His public relations men knew about it. The public knew about it—but not the billionaire.

After leaving Las Vegas, the aides halted Mell Stewart's practice of clipping newspapers for Hughes. The television reception in the Bahamas was poor, and Hughes gave up watching TV. He was in no condition, and hardly inclined, to stroll down to the Britannia Beach Hotel lobby and pick up a clutch of newspapers himself. What he knew about events beyond his little bedroom was what the aides decided he ought to know.

Eckersley's business venture involved a mining company called Pan American Mines Ltd. Eckersley was president of the firm. It was a newly organized company claiming to have valuable uranium and copper properties in Arizona. The stock was listed, however, on the Canadian Stock Exchange in Montreal, a trading center notorious for flimsy speculative stocks.

The stock prospectus, issued over the name of Eckersley as president, was liberally sprinkled with the name of Howard Hughes. It listed Eckersley as "Chief Personal Staff Executive to Howard Hughes," and gave his address as "Care of Howard Hughes" at the Britannia Beach Hotel. It listed Levar Myler, George Francom, and Kay Glenn as investing shareholders, and identified Myler and Francom as "Hughes Tool Co. staff executives" and Glenn as "Chief Executive, Hughes Production Co."

The first press release from Pan American Mines was headlined HOWARD HUGHES EXECUTIVES RECEIVE OK FROM QSC (Quebec Securities Commission). The public relations man who wrote it said later, "I became mesmerized like everyone else when they bandied about the Hughes name. I always felt—and was never led to believe otherwise—that Hughes was somehow involved."

So did the Canadian press and Canadian investors. Under the headline HUGHES INTERESTS ENTER QUEBEC PICTURE, the Montreal *Gazette* reported:

"Emissaries of the mysterious and enigmatic Hughes have been meeting with Quebec government and fiduciary figures on subjects related to their reported interest in becoming involved in the national resources picture in the province."

Canadian investors speculated that Hughes, having fled Nevada, might be headed north to sprinkle his wealth across the landscape there. When Pan American Mines stock went on sale, it shot up from its opening $1 per share to $5, and then skyrocketed to a giddy high of $12. In four months 972,999 shares were traded.

The liberal use of Hughes's name in the stock promotion prompted inquiries to Hughes officials by reporters. The officials called the new Hughes headquarters in the Bahamas and found themselves talking to Howard Eckersley rather than Howard Hughes. After a series of long and sometimes acrimonious conferences, they issued a terse statement for the aides asserting that "neither Hughes Tool Co. nor Howard Hughes has any interest in this venture. It is a private investment on their own *with approval of Hughes Tool*." Months later it was learned that this statement was not called to Hughes's attention. "Hughes Tools" was now approving projects without the knowledge of the owner of Hughes Tool.

Other than trailing the delicious—and fictitious— scent of Howard Hughes's millions, Pan American Mines was a scruffy little company. It had only $15 in cash in its till when its stock went on the exchange. Its "executive offices" were three tiny rooms behind a modest real-estate office in Phoenix, overlooking an alley. Vice-president of the firm was a longtime friend of Eckersley's, Floyd Bleak, a Flagstaff gravel-pit operator whose business had filed for federal receivership. Pan American Mines had no active mining under way. The stock prospectus claimed to have secured a million-dollar loan from a Phoenix insurance company to build an ore mill. The insurance company, upon investigation, turned out to have net assets of less than $190,000.

When these disturbing facts filtered up to Canada, the government ordered an investigation that rocked the Canadian Stock Exchange. Trading in the Pan American issue was halted, the chairman of the exchange was removed from office, and the stock brokerage house that underwrote the stock issue was forced to dissolve itself. At the height of the scandal the chairman of the Quebec province's security commission flew to Italy and resigned his office by cable.

Eckersley was finally forced to tell his billionaire employer about the Pan American Mines disaster when a Canadian warrant was issued for Eckersley in the case, a year after the issuance of the stock. "The Old Man really blew his cork," said a Hughes functionary familiar with the case. Shortly thereafter John Holmes was named chief senior aide and Eckersley dropped down to a plain senior aide. The Canadian charges against Eckersley were eventually dropped, but two of the stock promoters were convicted of fraud. In the end, the only other losers were the investors who had bought the 972,999 shares of Pan American Mines stock.

[ ]

While the air was leaking out of Eckersley's mining venture, another balloon was being pumped up. This one—the Clifford Irving hoax—involved Hughes much more intimately, and this time he was kept fully informed.

The Irving fraud had its genesis in the firing of

Bob Maheu. On the island of Ibiza, in the Mediterranean off the coast of Spain, Clifford Irving read about the noisy Nevada brannigan in a copy of *Newsweek.* Irving was a fiction writer, an expatriate New Yorker who was bored with a novel he was writing, bored with his marriage to his fourth wife, a German-born artist named Edith, and eager for something fresh and exciting.

Like Governor O'Callaghan, he perceived that the maneuvers of the Hughes Secrecy Machine made no sense if Hughes indeed was healthy, competent, and operative. Irving did not know what the Secrecy Machine was concealing, but it had to be something wrong with Hughes that was chronic, pitiable, or calamitous. Whatever it was, Irving saw in it a chance to have some fun and make some money.

He conceived the outrageous idea that he could fake Hughes's life story and pass it off as genuine. He concluded that Hughes could not effectively disavow it, either because he was dead, or a human vegetable, or too disabled to make a public appearance.

Newsweek carried a photo of a portion of the "Dear Chester and Bill" letter in Hughes's handwriting. Irving studied the sample carefully and practiced writing like Hughes. Then he faked a few letters from Hughes to himself, culminating in a suggestion that Irving was the writer who ought to be entrusted with producing Hughes's authorized biography.

Irving dangled this bait before his New York publisher, McGraw-Hill, and they rushed into his trap. They had published a number of his books, had given him a contract for future work, and they trusted him when he offered what promised to be an automatic best seller. Irving then closed off the normal editorial scrutiny that such a project would undergo by cloaking it in typical Hughesian secrecy. Only the top McGraw-Hill executives were to know about it, and Irving was to be the sole go-between with Hughes.

He forged a letter from Hughes approving the project and had the billionaire warning that "I wish there to be no publicity about this . . . for the time being, and I would view a breach of this request very unfavorably." The final agreement provided that Hughes was to be paid $500,000 by McGraw-Hill— through Irving—to "any bank account of H. R. Hughes," $100,000 in advance, $100,000 on completion of the research, and $300,000 when the manuscript was delivered and approved. So tightly held was the project that the contract did not identify Hughes and referred to him only as "Señor Octavio."

With the help of a fellow hoaxer, Richard Suskind, Irving slapped together a 230,000-word manuscript in eight months. In an improbable stroke of serendipity, Irving and Suskind blundered onto the unpublished first draft of the memoirs of Noah Dietrich, written by the author of this book. The Dietrich manuscript was covertly handed over to Irving by Stanley Meyer, a down-on-his-luck Hollywood producer who (1) knew Irving in the hoaxer's earlier days in Hollywood, (2) was pretending to market Dietrich's memoirs while (3) secretly feeding the memoirs to Greg Bautzer, Hughes's personal attorney.

Dietrich's memoirs gave Irving a skeleton of fact

on which to drape a Hughes that existed only in Irving's wildly inventive imagination. He had Hughes, for example, visiting Ernest Hemingway in Cuba and going skinny-dipping with the novelist in the waters of the Caribbean. (Hughes had no interest in Hemingway and was not a book-reader.) He invented an encounter between Hughes and Dr. Albert Schweitzer in Africa and had Hughes offended by the good doctor's "racism." (Hughes would have been inclined to agree with that fictional bias.) He had Hughes "exposing" his own $205,000 loan to Donald Nixon by leaking the details to Drew Pearson, when in fact Hughes threw the full power of his Secrecy Machine into a vain effort to suppress that story.

After acquiring the Dietrich memoirs, Irving converted the "authorized" Hughes biography into an "autobiography" and upped the price from $500,000 to $750,000. McGraw-Hill went along with this and on December 7, 1971, announced the forthcoming publication of the Hughes life story "in his own words," with "a commentary by Clifford Irving."

Now the years of deception, manipulation, and secrecy surrounding the billionaire bore fruit. Neither his spokesmen nor Hughes were able to shoot down the blatantly fake book. First the spokesman for Hughes Tool Co., disavowed the book. Officials at McGraw-Hill and at *Life* magazine—which had paid $250,000 for the condensation rights to the Irving fake—shrugged off this corporate denial. Of course the Hughes Tool Co. executives would deny the autobiography, they replied; Hughes simply hadn't let them in on his secret.

Then Hughes himself telephoned Frank McCulloch of *Time* magazine, the last newsman who had interviewed him in person back in 1958. Hughes convinced McCulloch that he was talking to the real Hughes, but he could not convince McCulloch that the Irving book was spurious. McCulloch was more impressed by the findings of two handwriting firms, who had certified that the forged letters from Hughes were authentic.

Finally, Hughes conducted his telephonic interview with seven newsmen, all of whom had known him in long-past days. He convinced all seven that they were talking to the genuine Howard Hughes. He told them the Irving book was faked and that he had never met or talked to Irving. His denial was front-page news across the country.

Hughes staged his end of the telephonic interview from the aides' Office at the Britannia Beach Hotel. It is significant that he did not publicly denounce the Irving fake until January 7, 1972, a full month after McGraw-Hill had announced its publication. His long silence undercut his credibility when he finally spoke out. Any other noted American businessman, subjected to such an outrage, would have repudiated it within hours. But Hughes's health was uncertain. He had long stretches of bad days, then an upswing, and then more bad days. He also had to prepare himself psychologically; he had not confronted the outside world, except by telephone, for many years.

From the vantage of hindsight, the most interesting portions of the interview were Hughes's descriptions of his state of health and general physical condition. Whatever his other frailties, he was still a master at dissembling.

"I keep in fair shape," Hughes smoothly replied when asked about his physical condition. "Not great, not as good as I should . . . I mean I'm not in any seriously disparaging—that's not the word. What the hell is the word I'm looking for? I'm not in any seriously derogatory—that's not the word either."

The disciples of Sigmund Freud would doubtless find these verbal slips revealing—that the first words he used in trying to describe himself were "disparaging" and "derogatory." He finally found something more appropriate. "I'm not in any serious deficient—now there's the word. I'm not seriously in a deficient condition."

He ridiculed the stories about his long fingernails. "I have always kept my fingernails a reasonable length," he said with a show of indignation. "I cut them with clippers, not with scissors and a nail file the way some people do . . . I take care of them the same way I always have, the same way I did when I went around the world and times when you have seen me, and at the time of the flight of the flying boat, and every other occasion I have come in contact with the press. I care for my fingernails in the same precise manner I always have in my life."

He spelled out his plans for the future, all but one of which proved illusory. He intended to return to Las Vegas. He would soon be giving some face-to-face interviews. He intended to have photographs taken and released to the press. The pictures would be distributed soon, and they would end all the nonsense about his deplorable condition. A year later, queried about what had happened to the promised photos, Hughes spokesman Hannah snapped, "He'll release them when he's good and ready."

He was definitely going to fly again. "It would be the best possible thing in the world for me," he said. "I have not only contemplated it but planned it definitely. And it will, I think, be the best conceivable therapy for me because—well, it's just something that I like doing rather than something I don't like doing."

Even this unprecedented telephonic interview failed at its intended purpose—to demolish the Irving fake. As a London *Times* team wrote in *Hoax*, a study of the Irving flimflam, "Howard Hughes was the only man in the world whose outright public denial of the authenticity of his autobiography could actually convince a skeptic that it must be genuine."

For a sizable segment of the public Hughes's denunciation of the Irving book raised more questions than it provided answers. There ensued a lively debate over whether the voice speaking from the Britannia Beach Hotel was that of Hughes. Irving encouraged the belief that it was not. "In my opinion," he said, "it was a damn good imitation of his voice as it may have been three or four years ago." He declared that the telephonic Hughes was not *his* Hughes, one of the lone nuggets of truth in his many utterances.

Irving was finally brought down early in 1972 by the press, which knocked the legs out from under his story of how he had put the "autobiography" together. The newsmen were assisted by a kiss-and-tell Danish singer, the Baroness Nina van Pallandt, who had accompanied Irving to Mexico when he purportedly was interviewing Hughes. She asserted that

Irving could not have met Hughes there, as he claimed, because he had spent all his time with her. Intertel agents established that the McGraw-Hill checks for "H. R. Hughes" had been deposited in a Swiss bank by one Helga R. Hughes, who turned out to be Irving's wife, Edith. McGraw-Hill and Time-Life finally branded the book a fake when this writer pointed out a long series of parallels between the Dietrich memoirs and the Irving manuscript, some of which bordered on plagiarism.

Gordon Margulis says that Hughes was not nearly as upset about the Irving hoax as were his lawyers and executives back in the States.

"He said a number of times that he didn't have anything much against Clifford Irving. As Hughes put it, 'He didn't get any of *my* money.' "

Davis and Gay had their own reasons for being upset with the Irving fraud. Irving maintained that Hughes had met him "in various motel rooms and parked cars throughout the Western Hemisphere"— at a time when Hughes was refusing to sit down with Nevada gambling authorities to iron out the snarls in his casino management. This offended the Nevada officials, already miffed at Hughes's lack of cooperation. Even the ultimate demolition of Irving brought little satisfaction to Davis and Gay. They had decided —because they wanted to believe it—that the mastermind behind Irving was Robert Maheu, and Maheu had been summoned before a New York grand jury for questioning about his knowledge of the hoax. He told the jury he knew nothing whatever about it.

"They [Davis and Gay] could not believe that their archenemy, Robert Maheu, was not somehow involved," wrote the authors of *Hoax*. "Their disappointment at his omission from the federal case can be compared to that of a James Bond addict who realizes toward the end of the latest Ian Fleming that Ernst Blofeld is not going to make an appearance."

If he could have known what he was setting into motion, Hughes would have been better off never to have staged his 1972 interview. The press would have shot down Irving in due course anyway. And the interview had two consequences no one envisioned.

It brought about Maheu's successful defamation suit, with its $2,800,000 judgment.

And all the publicity attracted the attention of Bahamian officials to their best-known but never-seen guest. This time, Hughes found himself dealing with an officialdom that insisted upon some answers.

[9]
ESCAPE

On the sunny afternoon of February 15, 1972, if any of the guests lounging around the pool of the Britannia Beach Hotel had lifted their gaze toward the top floor they would have observed an astonishing sight. They would have seen the richest man in the United States being hustled down the outdoor fire escape on a stretcher borne by three men.

Howard Hughes, proprietor of an international airline, sole stockholder of Hughes Tool Co., Nevada's number one gambling house owner, and the eighth largest U.S. defense contractor, was in frantic flight from the Bahamian immigration authorities. Even as his distraught aides were toting him down the fire escape, the Bahamian officials were entering the penthouse he had just fled.

Hughes's desperate plight had its origin in the

Clifford Irving hoax. On February 2, with the Irving controversy blazing merrily, the Honorable Cecil Wallace Whitfield, black leader of the Bahamian Free National Party, rose at his desk and directed a number of parliamentary questions to the government. They concerned the presence of Howard Hughes at the Britannia Beach Hotel, and were meant to find out whether he was complying with the Immigration Act, and whether the members of his entourage had obtained the work permits required of non-Bahamians gainfully employed in the Commonwealth. The Home Affairs Minister, Arthur Hannah, advised the honorable member that he would check into the matter and report back his findings.

Hughes's imperial attitude toward the laws and rules that bound others contributed to the *Perils of Pauline* cliffhanger in which he found himself. He had come, over the years, to regard himself as a sort of sovereign entity, entitled to diplomatic immunity. His view of himself was not without justification. If the governor of Nevada and the President of the United States bent or fractured their regulations to accommodate him, why should a little place like the Bahamas niggle?

Hughes did not even have a current U.S. passport. Renewing his long-lapsed passport would require him to submit a series of contemporary photographs. So "arrangements" were made and he traveled without a valid passport.

"None of us had Bahamian work permits," Margulis said. "We were told by the aides that the matter had been 'taken care of' and we didn't have to bother."

Hughes was not even a registered guest of the hotel where he had been living for more than fourteen months. If anyone asked at the desk of the Britannia Beach for Howard Hughes, the polite response was that there was no Howard Hughes registered. More persistent reporters, who discreetly obtained a look at the hotel records, found that this was true. His name was nowhere on the hotel register or on its billings.

But now he had announced to the world, in his telephonic interview, that he was living in the hotel, and the oppositionist Free National Party wanted assurances that he was toeing the laws of the Bahamian Commonwealth. When he had arrived in the islands, there had been a flurry of stories that he would be making heavy local investments. None had been forthcoming. To the rank-and-file blacks, Hughes was no great economic asset; he was just another rich "whitey" holed up in an expensive hotel.

The parliamentary questions were a touchy subject with the new black Prime Minister, Lynden Pindling. A few years earlier, his Progressive Liberal Party had toppled the whites from power in a rising tide of black discontent with the long rule of the white "Bay Street boys." His victory had been facilitated by a series of gamy scandals involving casino licensing and dissatisfaction with the colonial status of the island's black majority.

Pindling was a moderate, hardly the equivalent of a Bahamian Black Panther, and the FNP had raised a politically sensitive issue in Hughes's favored status. The Hughes party had been "stroking" Pindling, in keeping with their customary strategy toward those in power. They had made available to Pindling Chester Davis's leased yacht for Pindling's occasional use. Whatever gentling effect this had on Pindling's view of Hughes, it merely heightened the resentment of his political opponents.

On February 14 a group of Bahamian immigration officials visited the Hughes penthouse. They were turned away at the locked partition. They left visibly ruffled, trailing intimations that they would be back.

Shortly after this, urgent telephone calls were made from The Office in an attempt to pull some strings. The string-pulling didn't work.

At about 2:45 P.M. the next day Howard Eckersley sought out Gordon Margulis in a state of agitation. "He said we had to get Mr. Hughes out of the penthouse," recounted Margulis, "and we had to do it right away. He had word that the Bahamians were on their way to the hotel for a face-to-face meeting with the boss."

An Intertel agent had hastily scouted out a vacant room down on the sixth floor, the only one in the hotel. The agent had reserved the room in someone else's name.

"There wasn't any way we could get Mr. Hughes off the island or even out of the hotel," Margulis said. "We didn't have any contingency program, because no one had foreseen any trouble. All we could do was hide him in another room for the time being while we tried to throw together some escape plan."

The problem was to get Hughes down to the sixth-floor room unseen before the Bahamians came charging into the penthouse. The aides couldn't take him past the guard and down the elevator in broad daylight, because the Bahamians were closely monitoring the elevators.

Margulis joined Eckersley and Chuck Waldron in Hughes's bedroom. Hughes had been briefed on the problem and had delegated the solution to his aides.

"There was only one route we had open," said Margulis, "and that was down the outdoor fire escape. The fire escape was in plain view of the hotel pool and the grounds around the pool but we had no choice. So we put Mr. Hughes on a stretcher and out we went and down the fire escape."

Margulis said that the billionaire "was as cool as an ice cube." His only complaint was that the sun was too bright and hurt his eyes. "After all those years in a blacked-out room, I guess he was entitled to complain a little.

"It was a funny thing about the boss. He'd get very upset about some crises that really weren't crises except in his imagination. I mean like the bomb tests in Nevada. But when he was in a real touch-and-go, like in Nassau and in the Nicaragua earthquake, he kept his nerve. It seemed almost like he got a kick out of it.

"I wasn't so cool myself," Margulis said. "I had the front of the stretcher, with Eckersley and Waldron carrying the rear end of it. As we went out the ninth-floor fire door and started down the steps, I said to myself, *Don't slip, Gordon, or there goes a billion dollars.*"

The stretcher-bearers scanned the pool area, but no

one seemed to have spotted them. At the sixth floor, they ducked back into the hotel through the fire door. They deposited the supine billionaire in a narrow landing between the fire escape and the corridor door. There ensued a tangle of events that were straight out of a Feydeau bedroom farce.

Leaving Hughes and the two aides on the landing, Margulis eased out the door into the corridor to make sure it was clear of traffic.

"There were two problems," Margulis said. "Up the corridor were two maids' carts but no maids, which meant they were making up a room and could pop out at any moment. Down the corridor, toward the room where we were trying to take Mr. Hughes, the door of the adjoining room was standing open.

"So I sauntered down toward our room, trying to look casual. I looked in the room adjoining ours. The suite was occupied by a New York lawyer named Dick Wynn, his wife and daughter. I'd met them playing tennis. They knew I was with the Hughes party, and like everyone else, they were full of curiosity about Mr. Hughes."

Mrs. Wynn looked up and saw Margulis, and came out into the corridor.

"What a nice surprise, Gordon," Mrs. Wynn said. "What are you doing down on the sixth floor?"

Margulis improvised a story that he was looking for some friends who had just checked in. "I told her I couldn't find them," he said, "and then gave her a little wave and went on down toward the elevator as if I were leaving the floor. When I looked back, she had gone back into the room, but she had left the damn door open.

"I pussyfooted back up the corridor toward where we had stashed the boss, and this time the daughter came out. I told her it looked as if the elevator was busy, and said, 'I guess I'll just walk up.' So I gave *her* a little wave and went up the corridor and out the exit where Mr. Hughes was waiting."

"We got trouble," Margulis told Eckersley and Waldron. He explained that they were caught in the middle, between the maids on one side and the Wynns with their open door on the other. Hughes, without his hearing aid, couldn't hear Gordon's report.

"How are things going, Gordon?" he boomed out.

"He was talking much too loud and I made some shushing gestures," Margulis said. "He caught on right away, and gave me his OK sign—a circle with his first finger and thumb—to show me he understood."

Margulis, analyzing the problem, decided he had to get the Wynns' door closed. He went back down the corridor and rapped on the open door.

"The Wynns seemed surprised to see me again," Margulis said. " 'Oh, you're back again,' Mrs. Wynn said. 'Did you find your friends?' I told them not yet. Mr. Wynn was getting a massage from the hotel masseur. He told me that their TV set wasn't working, and that he was going to call a maintenance man. That was all we needed, someone else up on the sixth floor. I told him not to bother, that *I* knew a lot about TV sets and could probably fix it for them. I said I'd be right back as soon as I located my friends, and I walked out and closed their door behind me.

"I went racing down to the landing and told the aides to pick up the stretcher and get going, and I'd cover with the maids up the corridor. I went up and pulled their carts crosswise to block the corridor, and then stood there to block their view if they came out. Over my shoulder I saw Eckersley and Waldron trotting down the hall with Hughes, and into the new room. As soon as they were safe, I went scooting down to join them.

"Just then the Wynns' door opened, and out came Mrs. Wynn again. She said, 'You're a very busy man, Mr. Margulis.'

"I told her I had located my friends, and that they had the room next door. She said that was nice, and that she and her husband would like to meet them."

"Well, uh, maybe later," Gordon told her. "They're—uh—on their honeymoon and I don't think they'd like to be disturbed."

"Then I smiled and gave her another little wave, and ducked into the room. I sat down in a chair, my nerves tight as a banjo string. I thought, some day I'll be able to look back on this and think it was funny.

"The Old Man was very good, except that he kept forgetting and talked too loud. We kept shushing him, so the Wynns wouldn't hear him."

Margulis waited over an hour, and then went down to check the lobby. He found it swarming with Bahamian officials and police.

Meanwhile, on the ninth floor the guard had admitted the immigration officials just minutes after Hughes had been whisked down the fire escape. They had indicated that they would break down the partition if they weren't passed through. They made a search of the penthouse and found no Hughes. But they had picked up Rickard, Bundy, and Holmes without work permits. They escorted the trio to their rooms while they packed, and then took them to the airport for deportation. The sweep of the penthouse missed Mell Stewart and Dr. Clark, who had been over in Nassau at an art gallery.

After searching the penthouse, the Bahamians left and the partition door was again locked.

"Since they already had checked the penthouse," Margulis said, "we decided that was the safest place to keep Mr. Hughes while we figured out what to do."

They waited until after dark. Gordon checked the corridor again and found it all clear. They put Hughes on the stretcher, took him down the hall, and carried him back up the fire escape to the penthouse.

When they got him settled back in his bedroom, Hughes turned to Eckersley.

"I think I'd like to watch a movie now," he told his aide.

"That almost broke me up," said Margulis, "but Eckersley and Waldron didn't think it very funny. That was one of the few times that Mr. Hughes was firmly overruled by his senior aides."

Paradise Island is connected to Nassau by a bridge. The bridge is the only way off the island. The Hughes party had several planes at the Nassau airport but no way to get to them. The Bahamians knew that Hughes was still on Paradise Island, and they had the bridge under tight surveillance.

"They knew he was bottled up," said Margulis, "and they figured all they had to do was guard the bridge and wait until morning."

Stewart and Dr. Clark returned to the hotel from Nassau, unaware of what was going on. They were brought up to date.

Late in the evening the Hughes security officer, Jim Golden, made his way via the fire escape into the penthouse suite. Golden was a resourceful man, with useful connections. He had formerly been in the U.S. Secret Service, where he had been assigned to Richard Nixon when Nixon was Vice-President under Eisenhower. He had then joined Intertel, and later switched to the Hughes security team.

Golden had located a private boat, the eighty-three-foot *Cygnus*, anchored at Hurricane Hole on Paradise Island for repairs. Golden knew the captain, a man named Bob Rehak. The *Cygnus* was still being worked on, but was seaworthy. Golden said he would try to locate Rehak and charter the boat for a run to the Florida mainland.

Golden was a friend of Turner Shelton, U.S. Ambassador to Nicaragua. If they could get Hughes off Paradise Island, Golden thought he could arrange a new haven for him in Managua, capital of Nicaragua, under the protective wing of General Somoza, that country's dictator.

It was after midnight before Golden had completed his arrangements. Stewart and Dr. Clark joined the group in the penthouse, and the aides decided to put Operation Bug-out into action in the dark hours before dawn.

Shortly before 4 A.M. Howard Robard Hughes made his third trip on the Britannia Beach fire escape. In the tropical blackness, he was carried down the nine floors on a stretcher, accompanied by

Eckersley, Waldron, Dr. Clark, Stewart, and Margulis. The richest man in the United States departed his hotel by the classic route once used by flat-pocket vaudevillians unable to pay their hotel bills.

Hughes was loaded into a van behind the hotel. The party drove, with the van's lights off, out of the hotel grounds and down to the waiting *Cygnus*. Rehak and his mate, a man named Donald Hout, were waiting. This time the rituals were dispensed with and Hughes, clad only in pajama tops and his old bathrobe, was loaded into the wheelhouse, in full view of the two strangers.

A light rain was now falling. Golden stood on the dock and waved goodbye as the *Cygnus*'s engines turned over and it slipped out of its mooring. It moved down the channel under the Nassau bridge, only a few feet beneath the waiting Bahamian guards, and out into the open sea.

[ ]

"With the Hughes organization, it was women and children last," said Pat Margulis. Four years after the Britannia Beach fiasco, she still grows agitated and paces the floor in recalling what happened in Nassau to her and her then two-year-old son, Tiny. A slim, blue-eyed blonde who looks as if she stepped out of a Las Vegas chorus line, Pat is a former fashion model, a Catholic who attends Mass faithfully, an articulate woman with a mind of her own.

"I hadn't seen Gordon for two days when the Bahamians started rousting the Hughes party," she said. "I'd called the Britannia several times during the day, but the phone cable from Nassau over to

Paradise Island was out of order again. It was always breaking down, for some reason or other. I had a little company Toyota, but I didn't want to drive all the way over to the hotel if Gordon didn't have any time off. Tiny always got excited at the prospect of seeing Gordon and then if he didn't get to see him he'd throw a fit.

"About ten that night I was lying in bed, reading to Tiny, when there was a knock at my back door. I cranked the louvered window ajar and there was Fred Jayka. I let him in and he was very nervous, which wasn't like Fred at all.

"He threw two one-hundred-dollar bills on the bed and told me to get off the island as fast as I could, the first plane in the morning. I was stunned and asked him what on earth was going on."

Jayka told her that the Immigration officers were camped outside the locked partition at the Hughes penthouse, that they had impounded the known Hughes cars and boats, that they had already deported three aides, and that her husband and a few others were trapped with Hughes in the hotel.

"I got out down the fire escape," Jayka told her. "Gordon's worried sick about you and Tiny and wants you to barrel out of here as soon as possible. Your best chance is a flight to Miami, but take anything you can get off the island."

Jayka warned her that the airport was under close watch, and that the Bahamians had tried to pick up two Hughes workers for questioning while they were boarding a Miami plane. The men broke free and made it aboard the plane.

"He told me the Bahamians had the licenses of the

missing Hughes cars, and I couldn't use the Toyota or I'd get picked up. He took the keys to make sure I didn't use the car and then took off to go back and try to help Hughes.

"So there I was alone, scared, no car, with a baby. I called an English girl I'd met named Marie, who was married to an American who played in the band at the hotel. They came over in their car and brought some boxes so I could pack our belongings. Her husband had to play for the late show, but Marie came back and we drove over to the apartment where Hughes's pilots lived. We knocked and knocked on the door until a neighbor said they were gone, that they had fled that afternoon and left everything behind.

"Now I was frightened. I told myself, You're going to be the only one left on the island and you're going to wind up in Fox Hill. That's the Bahama prison, and I'd heard some awful stories about it."

That night Pat Margulis got no sleep. "I'd doze off and hear a noise and think the immigration people were coming for me."

There was a plane for Miami at noon, and Marie came to drive Pat and Tiny to the airport. Pat packed a single suitcase and left the rest of their possessions at the apartment.

"Marie carried Tiny and I went ahead and bought a ticket for Miami under the name of Mrs. King. I thought if they were looking for me they would be looking for a blonde with a baby, so I was going to be a blonde without a baby.

"I went through customs alone. The officer took a lot of time examining my luggage and eying me, and

I prayed he wouldn't ask for my passport. Tourists could fly back and forth to the mainland without passports. He finally passed me on through and Marie followed me with the baby.

"Just then I looked over and saw the tennis pro from the Britannia Beach hotel. He knew me and Gordon well, and he was a member of the Independence Party. He stood there glaring at me while I sat down and tried to act cool and unconcerned.

"Then they called the plane to Miami, and without looking back I got up and walked onto the plane alone. I sat there watching the boarding door and praying and pretty soon—God bless her—there came Marie carrying Tiny.

"She put him in my lap, leaned over and kissed me on the cheek and walked on off. Like the song says, she was one hell of a woman.

"I spent six hours in the Miami airport waiting for a plane to Vegas. I had a restless baby and no baby gear, and I didn't know where Gordon was, whether he was in Fox Hill, or whether he was even alive. I didn't find out what had happened until the next day in Las Vegas, and I didn't see Gordon again for four months, when I got to visit him up in Vancouver."

Pat Margulis shook her head angrily. "Sometimes people used to say how wonderful it was to be part of the Hughes organization.

"Whenever I heard that, I wanted to spit."

[ ]

The trip to the mainland took twenty-two hours. The sea was rough and the *Cygnus* pitched and rolled. After a while they took Hughes back into a stateroom and gave him some Dramamine to ward off seasickness, but he proved a good sailor and made the trip well.

Margulis fared much worse. The ship reeked of fresh paint and diesel oil, and within an hour Margulis was stricken with seasickness.

"I just stretched out on the floor of the storeroom and tried to tell myself that I wasn't going to die. After a while I didn't care if I did."

Hughes asked Eckersley, "What's Gordon doing on that floor? Floors are filthy, and he knows better than that."

"Tell him I know all that," Margulis told Eckersley. "And I'm not getting up."

As the day wore on, Margulis felt better and went up on deck. There was no food aboard, and only a part of a bottle of Poland water that someone had fetched along for Hughes. As they neared Florida, the sea smoothed out, and Rehak brought the *Cygnus* into Biscayne Bay and docked it at a luxurious house that Bill Gay had maintained there for a number of years.

"Gay was waiting there for us when we docked," Margulis recalled. "He told us, 'You fellows have done a splendid job and we're going to get some sandwiches for you.'"

Gay wanted Hughes moved into the house for a few days. Hughes needed some dental work, and Gay suggested that this would be a good opportunity to have it done.

"Hughes never liked that Florida house, and he refused to go into it," Margulis said. "Golden had made arrangements for us, and there was a U.S. Customs man waiting in Florida to pass us on through to Nicaragua.

"Gay kept talking about a stopover, but Mr. Hughes said to tell him there was no way he was going to stay in Florida. So we got another van and loaded the Old Man aboard and headed up to Fort Lauderdale. Waldron and I went in the van with Mr. Hughes, with Allen Stroud driving."

At the Fort Lauderdale airport, there was supposed to be a leased executive jet waiting. But there was a hitch, and the plane wasn't there when the Hughes van arrived.

Stroud didn't know what to do, so he kept driving around at random, anxiously looking for the jet to land. After a while, Hughes began to get irascible.

"Who's driving this contraption?" Hughes asked Margulis.

"Allen Stroud, one of the guys," Margulis said.

"Can he *see* me?" Hughes wanted to know.

"No, sir, he can't see you," Margulis said.

"Are we doing all right?"

"I think we are," Gordon said. "The plane will be in very soon."

"I'm glad to hear that," said Hughes, "because that's the *third* time we've passed that fucking airport tower."

"Just then the jet landed, and I pointed it out to Hughes," Margulis said.

"Well, bless us, we have a plane," said Hughes. "Now, do you think it might be possible for us to get *aboard* the plane?"

The van pulled out onto the runway, and one of

the aides went through the standard ritual. He shepherded the pilot and copilot out of the jet, took them about fifty yards from the plane and stationed them with their backs to it. Hughes was carried aboard and sequestered in the rear of the jet, and then the pilots were permitted to board. Margulis, Stewart, Dr. Clark, Waldron, and Eckersley piled in and off they went.

At Managua they took Hughes to the Intercontinental Hotel and Margulis and Waldron whisked him in the back way in a wheelchair without being spotted. They put him in a single room temporarily, because the hotel management hadn't had time to clear out the collection of suites the party required.

"We had to improvise everything because we had bugged out of the Bahamas at a dead run," Margulis said. "There hadn't been time for the usual advance work, and everyone was exhausted and groggy. Word leaked to the press that Hughes had arrived at the hotel, and reporters and photographers were combing the hotel looking for him."

There was one close call that sent shudders through the Hughes Secrecy Machine. One of the aides went out of Hughes's room on an urgent mission and left the door open. The billionaire was asleep on the bed, clad only in his shorts, in full view of the corridor.

"Down the hall came a reporter *and* a photographer," Margulis said. "If they had just glanced into the room, they could have got the first authentic photograph of Hughes in more than fifteen years.

"They went right on by, without realizing what they had missed. I guess they were looking for a room with a platoon of guards around it and figured that any room with a wide-open door couldn't have been Mr. Hughes's room."

After the customary frosty silence, Hughes spokesman Dick Hannah in Los Angeles confirmed to the news media that Howard Hughes had indeed departed the Bahamas and was now in residence in Nicaragua as a welcomed guest of the government. He gave no explanation for the departure and no details as to how the leavetaking had been accomplished. Perhaps he didn't know the spine-tingling details. Once the ordeal was over, the aides blotted the dreadful affair out of their minds, as if it had never happened.

Living together in a tight little world where they controlled all the information, the aides tended to take an Orwellian approach to events that got out of hand. If what had happened was embarrassing, they flushed it down the memory tube and revised reality.

Some months after Operation Bug-out, the captain and mate of the *Cygnus* gave a frank—and accurate —account to a Miami *Herald* reporter.

They described Hughes as "frail because of lack of activity," weighing about 120 pounds, with a long beard, hair down to his shoulders, and outsized toenails.

When the senior aides read the *Herald* account, they were outraged. "It's disgusting that the press can print *lies* like that and get away with it," said dour Levar Myler. "There ought to be some way to *prevent* such terrible stories."

"I was flabbergasted," Margulis said. "Both the

guys on the *Cygnus* had got a good look at the boss and simply told what they saw. The story was quite accurate, and I told Levar it was.

"He just glared at me, threw the paper down and walked away."

[10]
REACHING OUT

Unlike his close aides, Hughes seemed to get a lift in spirits from the telephonic interview and its unruly aftermath. He had enjoyed the give-and-take with the seven newsmen, his first contact with the press in fourteen years. He had been thrust out into broad daylight—if only on a hotel fire escape—and the sky hadn't fallen in on him. And two total strangers, the crew of the *Cygnus*, had got a close-up look at him and neither had jumped overboard.

"He began to sing a little, now and then," said Margulis. "And he hadn't sung since he left Las Vegas.

"He had only one song. It was that nonsense song from the early 1950's, 'Hey! Ba-ba-re-bop.' He'd sing it to himself, just that nonsense line over and over. 'Hey! Ba-ba-re-bop,' 'Hey! Ba-ba-re-bop.' It sounded pretty funny coming from him because he was not a man for nonsense, but I always kept a straight face. You knew he was feeling chipper about things when he started 'Ba-ba-re-bop'-ping. And that wasn't often."

Shortly after the wild dash to Nicaragua, Hughes got two pieces of good news. The U.S. Supreme Court announced that it would hear his appeal from the $145 million default judgment in the TWA case. The news was a last-minute reprieve, a lone ray of light after ten years of judicial gloom. Had the court refused to hear the appeal, the long, costly battle would have been over and lost. Now there was at least a last, slim chance to turn the case around.

"Hey! Ba-ba-re-bop."

Up in New York, Clifford Irving tossed in the towel and finally admitted that his McGraw-Hill autobiography was 24-karat brass. The Hughes organization had spent a huge sum of money—well over $200,000—trying to shoot down the fake because of the bad vibrations it had sent through the Nevada gaming authorities. Now at least the Nevadans knew that Hughes hadn't been cavorting around the country with Clifford Irving, and maybe the long-stalled casino reorganization could move forward.

Hughes stayed on in Nicaragua less than a month, although he found the little Latin American dictatorship a pleasant and compatible place. There were no embarrassing parliamentary demands about such things as work permits and passports. There was no parliament in Nicaragua.

But the country had one drawback. The telephone

system was atrocious. Communication between Hughes's entourage and the California control center was a constant problem, and in March plans were made to move on up to Vancouver.

In his final week in Nicaragua, Hughes made a momentous decision. In his constricted world, it was comparable to Columbus deciding to sail out into the unknown great sea to hunt for the Indies, or, at the very least, Lady Godiva's decision to ride naked through the streets of Coventry.

After more than ten years of invisibility, Hughes decided to materialize in the flesh and meet two human beings face to face.

The men who had piloted the *Cygnus* had seen him, of course, but that had been mere happenstance, unavoidable during his wild, unplanned flight. He now consciously decided to sit down with two outsiders.

What fetched the billionaire up from the depths of his personal Loch Ness was a message from Anastasio Somoza, El Presidente of Nicaragua. The message, relayed to the Hughes headquarters via Ambassador Turner Shelton, was that El Presidente would be pleased and honored to meet with Mr. Hughes, if only for an exchange of pleasantries and a short chat.

Hughes told the aides that he just might grant the audience. Some of the aides were upset. If he started meeting with outsiders, where would it all lead? If Hughes re-entered the world, their control over him would end and so would their reason for existence.

On the other hand, no one was about to tell the billionaire that he couldn't do whatever he wanted to do. So the aides talked unhappily among themselves and hoped their employer would abandon this wild notion of behaving normally.

Then one day Hughes sent word that he wanted to be barbered and groomed. Mell Stewart brought in his tools and set about lopping the great fall of hair and the straggling beard. Margulis accompanied Stewart, and this displeased Hughes.

"What's Gordon doing in here?" Hughes demanded.

"He's going to help me," Stewart replied.

"But Gordon handles the *food*," Hughes complained. "We don't want my food handler in here when I'm getting my hair cut."

"Mr. Hughes, haven't you ever heard of *soap and water*?" Stewart asked in exasperation. "When he's through here, Gordon goes and *washes up*."

Grooming Hughes in Nicaragua took longer than usual. Other than minor mustache trimming, Hughes hadn't been barbered for three or four years. One of his oddities was that he never made any reference to —or explanation of—his long periods of self-neglect. Neither did his aides. It was a subject that was not discussed, the way a close family might ignore a behavioral peculiarity of a distinctly eccentric but very rich uncle.

"The only time the matter came up," said Mell Stewart, "was now and then when Hughes would complain that his untrimmed mustache gave him problems in eating.

"I'd tell him, 'I can take care of that in a few minutes with my barber scissors.' And he'd usually say, 'Well, all right—but not today. I've got other things to do.' "

When they trimmed his nails, Hughes insisted that they leave his left thumbnail about a half-inch long and squared off.

"That's my screwdriver," he said. "Don't trim my screwdriver too short." He used his thumbnail to flick pages in his documents, and to tighten loose screws or make adjustments in his movie sound equipment or other appliances.

"The only reason I could figure out why he used his thumbnail," said Margulis, "was that it did away with handling a screwdriver, which might have germs on it.

"Handling inanimate objects had developed into a complicated ritual. When you were going to bring him a spoon, for example, the spoon handle had to be wrapped in Kleenex and Scotch-taped. Then you would take another piece of Kleenex to hold the Kleenex wrapping, so the wrapping wouldn't get contaminated. He would lift the wrapped spoon off the piece of Kleenex you were holding it with. So you can see what a problem it would have been whenever he needed a screwdriver."

"He looked like a different man when we got him shaved and barbered and groomed," said Stewart. "It made you wonder why he let himself go for so long."

The audience with Somoza and Ambassador Turner took place aboard the Hughes executive jet at the airport. Hughes was removed from the hotel in a wheelchair, taken to the airport, and put aboard the plane before his visitors arrived. He was accompanied by Margulis, Myler, Holmes, and Francom.

He greeted the President of Nicaragua and the U.S. Ambassador wearing his pajama bottoms, his bathrobe and his old sandals.

The tall, emaciated billionaire and the stocky, bespectacled dictator hit it off well. They had much in common; in many ways their coming together was comparable to a state visit between two sovereigns.

Somoza had become the permanent El Presidente of Nicaragua back in 1967, and he had exercised much the same absolute power over his country that Hughes had exercised over *his* empire. Nicaragua was the most highly Americanized of Latin American countries. Somoza came from a conservative coffee-plantation family. His father, also named Anastasio, had been President from 1937 until 1956, when he was assassinated. The elder Somoza had been educated at Pierce Commercial College in Philadelphia and had graduated from West Point. He had then spent several years working in the United States as an auditor for an automobile company. He had returned to his native land with a boundless enthusiasm for certain Yanqui institutions. These included baseball, which he introduced in Nicaragua, and unfettered private enterprise, which he exercised mainly in behalf of the Somoza family. His ascendancy to power had been accomplished in an election closely monitored by a sizable force of U.S. Marines. When he became El Presidente, in the depths of the Depression, the going rate for a policeman or a skilled chef in Nicaragua was about $4 a month. The elder Somoza drew $100,000 a year and, not unexpectedly, his son shared Hughes's staunch anticommunism.

The meeting lasted some forty-five minutes. As the conversation went on, the senior aides began to get restless, and Somoza said that he did not want to hold up their departure.

"Don't worry about it," said Hughes. "This plane isn't going to go anywhere until I'm ready."

Hughes made one gaffe that Somoza diplomatically overlooked.

After they had talked a while, Hughes looked at his guest quizzically and remarked:

"You know, you speak English very well for a foreigner."

El Presidente did not remind Hughes that he had been educated in the United States, or that, in Nicaragua, it was *Hughes* who was the foreigner.

One of the rewarding by-products of the meeting, from the viewpoint of the Hughes Secrecy Machine, was an interview Ambassador Shelton gave the press after Hughes's departure.

"I noticed no difficulty in his hearing and his voice was strong," the ambassador said. "He was in good humor and thanked me for helping make arrangements for his visit here. His hair was cut short like he used to wear it. He shook hands with both of us, and had a firm handshake.

"It is absolutely nonsense what has been printed about his nails being as long as Fu Manchu's. His fingernails were as well-manicured as yours or mine."

Some skeptics pounced upon Shelton's reference to the "firm handshake" as immutable evidence that Somoza and Shelton had met a Hughes double, not the real billionaire. The real Hughes, they asserted, would have recoiled from an outthrust hand as if it were a poisonous asp. Ergo, *voilà*, Q.E.D., it was not Hughes who granted the unprecedented audience.

Margulis, who was present, confirms that the real Hughes gave Somoza and Turner a real handshake. Two each, in fact. One when they boarded the plane, another when they departed. The point about Hughes that escaped the skeptics was that there was never anything immutable about him; his only predictable quality was that he was highly unpredictable. "He not only shook their hands," said Margulis. "He didn't even wince."

During his conversation with his visitors, Hughes volunteered an explanation of his legendary reclusiveness and how it had developed.

"He explained to us," Ambassador Shelton told reporters later, "that he had slipped gradually into the isolation picture because he was a compulsive worker who was constantly being interrupted by telephone calls and unwanted visits. He said he worked almost compulsively up to eighteen hours a day and found he was getting thirty or more interruptions and discovered that almost none of them accomplished anything but to waste his time.

"So he told his aides to screen the calls and found that he liked it when the calls were reduced to zero."

This explanation presented to the outside world, under the imprimatur of a U.S. ambassador, an image of Hughes that must have delighted his public relations men. The world never saw him because he was intensely occupied, through marathon sessions, with the affairs of his vast empire. He was a man in charge, coping with such heavy responsibilities that he permitted no distractions. On the testimony of a man who had seen and talked to him, Howard Hughes was simply a well-manicured devotee of the Protestant work ethic, with a neatly barbered Vandyke beard.

At the conclusion of the airport conference, Somoza gave Hughes a special gold coin as a memento of his stay in Nicaragua, and invited him to return. Then his visitors departed, and the plane took off for Vancouver.

In four short weeks, Hughes had seen *four* total strangers from the fearsome outside world, and nothing disastrous had happened. He was becoming —for Hughes—a social gadabout.

The jet landed at Vancouver in the early daylight hours, in a heavy rain. This time the advance work had been done properly. Canadian officials were waiting to check the party into the country without intruding upon its principal. "We had nothing to ask," said one official stiffly. "We were aware of his identity, and of the fact that he and his colleagues were self-supporting and not likely to become charges of the welfare services."

Hughes was transferred from the plane to a waiting car in a wheelchair and driven to a rear entrance of the Bayshore Inn, overlooking the Vancouver harbor.

"In spite of the miserable weather, the boss was in an upbeat mood," said Margulis. "When we got to the hotel, I started to get the wheelchair out of the car trunk.

"He said, 'Don't bother. I'm going to walk in.'

"With Francom on one side of him and me on the other, he just *walked* into the hotel like anybody else. Took his time, too.

228

"In the foyer there was a middle-aged lady, and over at one side a fellow cleaning the windows," Margulis said. "Normally that would have thrown him into a panic, but he just stopped and looked around."

"This is pretty nice," Hughes said.

One of the aides told Margulis, "Get the wheelchair and get him moving."

"I told him to ease off and let the boss look around a little bit."

When they took Hughes up the elevator to the suite they had picked out for him, Hughes went over to the window and looked out, instead of scuttling into his bedroom.

"The aides had picked the big middle room for The Office," Margulis said. "The boss gazed out the window awhile and watched a seaplane landing in the harbor. He said he liked the view.

"The aides didn't like that one bit," said Margulis. "They told me to get him away from the window and into his bedroom.

"Then something happened that really frosted me. The boss said he liked the big room and the view and said it would make a nice sitting room for him. He hadn't had a sitting room for years, and he'd always had the windows taped and never looked out.

"They warned him that somebody could fly past the sitting room in a helicopter and shoot his picture with a telephoto lens. 'Here's *your* room,' they told him, and took him into another little blacked-out bedroom, with the draperies all taped down tight. He just went along with them, and they had him back in his cave again. After a while he got into bed, and called for a movie, and everything was just the way it had been for years."

But to the outside world, the fiction was cultivated that Hughes was moving out of isolation. In April, Eckersley told a Vancouver reporter that Hughes would shortly be releasing the contemporary photographs he had promised. A Hughes publicist said that the picture-taking project was moving ahead, that three photographers were under consideration for the historic portrait, and that one fine day soon the public would be shown a photograph of the invisible man.

A year later there were still no pictures. No official photograph of Hughes was ever released.

Among those curious about what Hughes looked like were some people high in the inner circle. They included Kay Glenn, the operative executive for the entourage.

In 1971 *Look* magazine ran an article about Hughes and put an artist's concept of the billionaire on its cover. It showed him with long hair down his back like a hippie.

Kay Glenn bought a copy of *Look*, and later questioned Margulis.

"That sketch of Hughes," he said. "Is that how he looks?" It was a tribute to the efficiency of the Secrecy Machine that even its overseer didn't know what the billionaire looked like.

Margulis says that the sketch was a remarkably accurate portrait. "But I didn't think it was any of Kay Glenn's business, so I told him hell, no. That turned out to be a good answer. When the boss got barbered in Nicaragua, he *didn't* look like the *Look* sketch."

Glenn finally got a look at his employer in Vancouver.

"Glenn was waiting at the hotel when we arrived," Margulis said. "He'd done some of the advance work there. When we came in from the ariport, he was at the door when we brought the boss in.

"He said, 'Good morning, Mr. Hughes.'"

Hughes asked Gordon, "Who was *that* fellow?"

"That was Kay Glenn," Margulis said.

"Kay Glenn? Oh, I remember him," said Hughes. "He's the fellow who fetches my movies for me."

[ ]

The Hughes entourage had now grown until it required twenty-four rooms at the Bayshore Inn. Not all of them were occupied. The party had the entire twentieth floor of the Inn, plus strategic rooms on the nineteenth directly below the Hughes suite. These were empty and locked, in keeping with the security routine of providing a "buffer zone" against any electronic eavesdropping. One Vancouver newspaper, reporting on these precautions, observed that the security surrounding the billionaire was considerably tighter than that protecting Canadian Prime Minister Trudeau on a recent visit to Vancouver.

One of the reasons for the Hughes party's apprehension was the large number of U.S. draft evaders who had crossed the border into Vancouver. Among the more militant, the unpopularity of the Vietnam war attached to anyone who profited from it, and both Hughes Aircraft and the helicopter division had extensive military contracts.

"We had one bomb scare," Margulis recalls. "One

day Fred Jayka and I came down together and the hotel doorman stopped us. He said he had seen a fellow put something in the back seat of one of the Hughes cars in the parking lot.

"Fred and I went over and took a look. There was a bag just inside the back door. Whoever had put it in there had pushed the button down to lock the door, which made it look suspicious.

"I took a quick look at the parking lot, and it was empty. So I reached over the front seat, picked up the bag and threw it as hard as I could out into the middle of the parking lot, while Fred and I fell flat to escape the concussion.

"Only there wasn't any concussion. I got up, feeling a little silly. 'I don't think that was a bomb,' I told Jayka. 'If it was, it was an awfully light bomb.'

"We went over and took a look at the package. It was filled with someone's dirty laundry."

The Hughes party stayed in Vancouver six months. During this period the impasse between the Hughes organization and the state of Nevada congealed and became set in concrete.

Supported by Governor O'Callaghan, Gaming Control Board Chairman Phil Hannifin demanded a face-to-face meeting with Hughes as a condition for approving the reorganization of the Hughes casinos. One sticking point was the licensing of Chester Davis, who had been elevated to the Toolco board of directors. The state law required that Davis, as a Toolco director, pass the licensing procedure. His name was duly submitted as a licensee, but the board refused to approve it. The O'Callaghan administration took the legally impeccable but hitherto unprecedented position that Hughes had to conform with the law just like any other casino owner. If Hughes wanted Chester Davis on the license, Hughes would have to say so in person, and a letter wouldn't do it.

"We're just trying to make sure," said the governor, "that Howard Hughes knows what is going on."

The concessions made to Hughes in the past, said Hannifin, "have diminished the integrity and dignity of the State of Nevada.

"Recent court proceedings in the Clifford Irving fraud case cast doubt on whether the handwriting of Hughes could be accepted as proof of his desires."

Trying to establish contact with Mr. Hughes, Hannifin declared, is "like yelling into a big barrel. All I ever hear is my own voice. And I'm not going up to Vancouver and sit on my duff until he agrees to see me."

At one point Bill Gay, Chester Davis, and other Hughes officials trooped up to Carson City to try to persuade the governor to bend the regulations slightly to accommodate the billionaire. The governor told the group that if they wished to discuss the Hughes licensing problems with him, Chester Davis could not be present. Mr. Davis, the governor pointed out, was not on the Hughes license and therefore was not a proper participant in the discussions. Davis sat outside in the waiting room while the governor spelled out his position—the gaming board would act only after a face-to-face meeting with Hughes.

The hitherto irresistible Hughes organization apparently had encountered an immovable object. The Hughes attorneys could hardly argue, as they had in the TWA litigation, that Hughes declined to meet with *anyone*. If he could sit and chat with a Latin American dictator, it was difficult to explain why he could not sit down with the duly elected officials of Nevada.

While the Hughes organization wrestled with the problem of a governor who insisted on seeing Hughes, it received another request for an audience with the billionaire. One day an emissary dressed as Mickey Mouse showed up at the Bayshore Inn and sent word up to the suite that he had a present for Mr. Hughes. The caller was a member of the Walt Disney "Disney on Parade" group on a promotional tour and he sought to present Hughes with an authentic, inscribed Mickey Mouse watch. The inscription read: "While living legends must continually play cat and mouse with the public to retain credibility, I'm sure that even you must periodically wonder what time it is."

America's favorite cartoon character met the same blank wall that had stopped the TWA sleuths, the court process servers and all the rest. Mickey had to leave the watch with a functionary.

While Hughes was notoriously scornful of the time of day, he had an exquisitely sensitive awareness of time insofar as it affected his tax liabilities. The Canadian government granted visitors a six-month grace period from local tax laws. He had arrived in Canada on March 12, 1972, and his tax-free status expired on September 12 of that year.

Two weeks before this grace period expired, the entourage got word that Hughes was leaving Canada. The party would return to Nicaragua, where there were no local tax problems.

Two weeks before Hughes's tax exemption ran

out, the party packed and went back to the humid little Latin American country.

"At the Vancouver airport there was a foul-up," Margulis said. "Whenever we flew anywhere, the boss had to have a supply of chicken sandwiches and milk. He always did things the same way. Long ago, when he was setting airplane speed records and flying around the world, he stocked his planes with chicken sandwiches and milk. So it was a standing rule that we have the same provisions aboard the plane.

"They were taxiing the plane out to the runway when I checked the supplies. Someone had screwed up, and there was no bread aboard for the chicken sandwiches. I bucked the crisis up the line to Levar Myler, and they stopped the plane. They lowered the exit steps, and Richard disembarked, flagged down an airport car and went off somewhere to get a loaf of bread. The car came racing back with Richard and the bread, and he hopped aboard and off we went to Nicaragua."

At Nicaragua there occurred a foul-up of somewhat graver dimensions. Hughes decided to sell off Hughes Tool Co.—and underpriced the stock by $300 million.

[11]
EARTHQUAKE

Hughes's sudden decision to sell Hughes Tool Co. was an act of desperation and, ironically, an unnecessary one. He disposed of the great money machine, which had nourished his empire for almost a half-century, in order to raise money for the TWA judgment against him. Then, when he had the money in hand to pay off TWA, the U.S. Supreme Court astonished everyone and threw out the judgment.

By 1972 the TWA judgment had risen, because of accumulated interest, to $170,000,000. Hughes had lost the legal struggle in every jurisdiction for more than ten years. The case had been litigated exhaustively and, except for Chester Davis, no one expected the high court to overturn ten years of adverse judicial rulings.

Hughes was convinced that he would shortly have

to come up with $170,000,000 in cash. And Hughes didn't have $170,000,000.

How could a man worth more than a billion dollars be in a bind for a mere $170 million? The answer was that Hughes didn't keep large sums of idle money lying around. If he had, he would never have become a billionaire in the first place.

Hughes's billion consisted of his string of Las Vegas resorts, his Hughes Tool Co., his Hughes Air West, his helicopter manufacturing division, a half-dozen other enterprises, and vast stretches of undeveloped land. When the value of all these holdings was totaled, it came to something in the area of $1,250,000,000. But that was value, not money.

Hughes never had any personal attachment to mere money, à la Silas Marner. One of the better-founded legends about him, from the days when he moved about the outside world, had him frequently borrowing small change from his associates. In his pre-recluse days, he carefully cultivated the stories that he never carried cash, to discourage the notion that anyone could get rich by putting a gun in his ribs.

He not only didn't carry money, he avoided having any extensive sums accumulate in his name. Throughout the 1950's, his only personal source of income was $50,000 a year as president of Hughes Tool Co. He resigned that office at the outset of the TWA battle, to give himself legal immunity from subpoena. From about 1960 on, he drew no salary whatever from any of his enterprises.

When one is very rich, it is simple to live well without money. For many years, his organization maintained a bank account at the South Hollywood branch of the Bank of America under the name of the L.M. Company. The L.M. stood for Lee Murrin, a soft-spoken, mild-mannered functionary with Hughes Productions, the inactive moviemaking company headquartered at the Romaine center. Lee Murrin was Hughes's personal moneyman, a sort of walking Carte Blanche card. There wasn't any "L.M. Company" as such, only a bank account. In the course of a deposition about Hughes's financial affairs, Murrin was once asked to describe the L.M. Company. He said, "It is a . . . well, I don't know."

Hughes's bills—and, before the divorce, those of Jean Peters—were sent to Romaine for payment. Murrin paid them out of the L.M. Company account. The L.M. account was periodically replenished with funds sent up from another bank account in Houston. At the end of the year, a Hughes tax lawyer would sit down with an Internal Revenue Service agent and sort out which of the bills were deductible as a business expense and which were Hughes's personal liability. The personal bills were than added up, and Hughes Tool Co. would declare a dividend for its lone stockholder to take care of them.

He thus kept his personal—as opposed to corporate—income to a minimum. Noah Dietrich declared that in the 1950's, when Hughes Tool Co. profits soared far into the millions annually, Hughes on occasion paid a personal income tax of less than $20,000 a year. His companies grew richer and richer, but this burgeoning wealth was not reflected in Hughes's personal income. The niggardliness of his companies toward their proprietor was Hughes's own policy; he was content with the knowledge that their swelling assets, in the final accounting, all belonged to him.

When he faced the unhappy prospect of paying out $170,000,000 to TWA, his only recourse was to borrow the money or sell off some of his holdings.

In deciding which of his blue chips to cash in, he had only three options. He could sell his father's toolbit company, his land holdings, or his Las Vegas casinos. His immensely profitable Hughes Aircraft was no longer available for conversion into cash. After the disastrous internal revolt of the early 1950's, he had put all the stock of Hughes Aircraft into his Howard Hughes Medical Institute. Although Hughes was the lone trustee of the medical institute, it had been granted a nonprofit tax status and he could not retrieve the stock and sell it for his personal use.

His decision to sell off Toolco was foreshadowed in a memo he wrote to Maheu in 1969. He told Maheu then that he intended to retain his casinos "permanently."

"I have decided this once and for all," Hughes wrote. "I want to acquire even more hotels and to build this operation to be the greatest thing in the U.S. This is a business that appeals to me." The casinos were *his* acquisition; Toolco was his father's monument.

What he put on the market was the original Hughes Tool Co., not the Hughes Tool Co. of 1972. Hughes Tool Co. had become the umbrella company which held the bulk of his other enterprises, and his father's company was now merely the drilling-bit "division." He spun off the Houston-based drilling-bit enterprise, and formed a new umbrella company to take over his other holdings. But he let the "Hughes Tool Co."

name go with the drilling-bit division. To replace it and hold his other enterprises, a new umbrella company named Summa Corporation was formed.

The Toolco sale and the creation of Summa raise questions about the status of Hughes's financial judgment and his control over his own affairs.

Five million shares of the new drilling-bit "Hughes Tool Co." were put on sale at $30 per share. In less than a year the stock rose to $75 on the New York Stock Exchange. It went on to top $100, and then was split two shares for one. In 1976 the stock—adjusted for the split—has swung narrowly between $95 and $105 per original share.

Whatever his other frailties, as late as his Las Vegas period Hughes had been a sharp negotiator. As one writer phrased it, "He had the mind of a hostile pawnbroker." When the $30 price was suggested to him, he had weakly protested that it "ought to be at least 32," and then had given in.

His gross miscalculation of the true worth of Toolco was all the more puzzling because, in the mid-1950's, Noah Dietrich had canvassed the financial community and come up with a ball-park estimate of the company's worth. Hughes periodically "counted his chips" by tentatively sounding out potential buyers on what they would offer for one of his holdings.

Dietrich had reported back to Hughes that Toolco would bring between $350,000,000 and $400,000,-000. This estimate coincides closely with the market value Toolco established after the sale. Moreover, in 1972 the impending energy crisis, plus a brilliant new drilling-bit improvement—a "journal bearing" that substantially increased the drilling life of the bit—foreshadowed an upturn in profits. In the year after he sold Toolco, its profits more than doubled, and the stock became one of the New York Stock Exchange's hottest "glamour" issues.

"What I know about stocks and finances you can stick in the corner of a gnat's eye," said Gordon Margulis. "But Jack Real is a sharp businessman, and he was very upset about the Hughes Tool Co. sale.

"Jack took me to one side after Hughes signed the papers to sell off Hughes Tool. Jack said, 'We have just seen the financial rape of the twentieth century.' He predicted, on the day of the sale, that the stock would triple in value."

After the Hughes holdings were transferred to Summa, Summa then spun off the drilling-bit division, granted it the name of Hughes Tool Co., and the public stock sale was handled by the nationally known brokerage house of Merrill Lynch, Pierce, Fenner and Smith.

According to *Fortune* magazine, two representatives of Merrill Lynch, Julius Sedlmayr and Courtney Ivey, flew to Nicaragua on September 26, 1972, to verify that Hughes personally approved the transaction. Margulis was on home leave, and Stewart was off duty on that day, and neither witnessed the encounter.

But the *Fortune* account bears out what both Margulis and Stewart had observed. Ever since Hughes was thrust out of isolation by the Nassau uproar, he had been reaching out for wider human contact. The wild dash out into broad daylight on the Britannia Beach fire escape and the trip on the *Cygnus*, in full sight of two strangers, apparently had loosened the self-imposed bonds that had chained him to a little room for many years. There had been his unprecedented meeting with Somoza and Shelton, his leisurely stroll through the Vancouver lobby, and his abortive effort to acquire a sitting room with an outside view at the Bayshore Inn.

According to *Fortune*, after Hughes verified that he had approved the Hughes Tool sale, he was reluctant to let his visitors leave.

"For forty-five minutes," *Fortune* reported, "while they fidgeted and worried that they would miss their flight back to New York, Hughes talked about Hughes Tool Co. with what at times struck his listeners as nostalgia . . . He talked on about the company and its bright prospects until Sedlmayr insisted that he and Ivey really had to leave. Hughes offered to bring a plane down from Miami if they would visit longer, but they refused."

As they rose to leave, Hughes once more defied one of his longest phobias. Again, he shook the hands of two visitors from the germ-laden outside world.

When the Hughes Tool sale and the creation of Summa were announced, the choice of the new name for the parent holding company puzzled those familiar with Hughes's quirks. "Summa" derives from the Latin, meaning the peak or top, and it did not sound like Hughes. He characteristically attached his own name to his enterprises—Hughes Aircraft, Hughes Air West, Hughes Sports Network, Hughes Helicopters, Hughes Nevada Operations.

This oddity was soon explained. Hughes hadn't picked the name for the company that would hold all his properties—in fact, he disliked the name "Summa" intensely. The name had been chosen by the Gay-Henley-Davis power group that were running his affairs.

"Right off, the boss said, 'I don't like that god-gamn "Summa" name,'" Margulis said. "He complained about it repeatedly. In fact, he told the aides that he didn't want any big supply of Summa letterheads printed, because he was going to change it."

Months later, when he met with Governor O'Callaghan and Gaming Director Hannifin in London, Hughes was still complaining about the name. "I don't like that name," he told his visitors.

It was not characteristic of Howard Hughes to put up with something that he didn't like. But in spite of his antagonism the name "Summa" somehow managed to survive Howard Hughes.

Within weeks after the visit from the Merrill-Lynch officials, Hughes again reached out for human contact. He sent word up to Nevada that he would yield to Governor O'Callaghan's demand that he spell out, in a face-to-face meeting, how he wanted his casinos licensed and who he wanted on the licenses. He asked only that the meeting be held in Nicaragua, pleading frail health. The expenses for the trip to Nicaragua would be borne, properly, by the Hughes organization. By Nevada regulations, all costs connected with licensing a casino operator are charged to the applicant. It was a major about-face for Hughes—or at least from the position that had been attributed to Hughes by his representatives.

When the offer was relayed to Governor O'Callaghan, he merely took it under consideration. He wanted the Hughes impasse—now well into its second year—resolved. But he was also concerned with maintaining the rectitude of the state of Nevada vis-à-vis Hughes, which had been impaired by the previous fawning on the billionaire. The governor had no objection to accommodating Hughes if traveling to Carson City imposed any real trauma on the billionaire. But the governor had reservations about meeting him under the aegis of a Latin American dictator.

On December 23, this unresolved issue was rendered moot. The Nicaraguan capital of Managua was rocked by a massive earthquake that leveled much of the city. The death toll ran into the thousands and for twenty-four hours no one outside Managua knew whether the victims included Managua's best-known guest.

Mell Stewart, a devout Mormon, had said his prayers and climbed into bed at the Intercontinental Hotel on the floor below Hughes's suite. The next day was Hughes's sixty-seventh birthday. Stewart wondered about getting his employer some small gift, or maybe a birthday card, and then dismissed the idea. Hughes didn't like birthdays; he didn't pay any attention to his aides' birthdays and he didn't like to be reminded of his own.

"All of a sudden I heard this deep roar or rumble that got louder and louder," Stewart recalled. "Then the room heaved and the water pitcher came sailing across the room and I was thrown out of bed. I staggered to the window and looked out. The whole hotel was shaking and heaving, and it was a very solidly built building. I grabbed my glasses and put on one shoe and tried to switch the lights on. The lights and the whole hotel power system were gone. I lit a candle, found my other shoe and got dressed and headed for the boss's suite. My hotel door was jammed shut and wouldn't budge. I backed off and kicked it down and sprinted for the stairs.

"There were a lot of airline stewardesses in the hotel," Stewart said. "I never saw so many undressed girls running around in my life."

The senior aide on duty was Jim Rickard. "Take care of the boss," he told Stewart. "I'm going to check on my family." Rickard and three of the other aides had their wives or members of their families visiting them.

Hughes had narrowly escaped injury when the quake toppled his movie sound amplifier. Rickard had caught it just as it was about to fall on the billionaire.

"Hughes was lying in bed naked," Stewart said. "The room was still heaving and it felt as if the hotel was going to collapse in a heap.

"The boss had to be the calmest man in Managua. He kept saying that he would be all right. He didn't show any anxiety about getting out of the hotel. He asked me, 'What is the extent of the damage?'

"I dashed to the window, looked out, and told him the whole town was falling down. I don't know whether he didn't hear me or didn't understand, but this didn't seem to bother him. He said something about watching a movie."

Stewart tried to get the naked billionaire dressed, but couldn't find any of his drawstring shorts. Hughes kept saying that he was all right, he'd borrow Stewart's underwear.

"I yelled at him that mine wouldn't fit him,"

Stewart said. "We could have put two Hugheses in one pair of my shorts."

Some of the other aides came up to the suite and an argument developed about whether to take Hughes out into the open. Then one of the hotel people came up and said everyone would have to evacuate the hotel at once.

Stewart finally located a pair of shorts, Hughes's old bathrobe and his sandals, and got the emaciated billionaire dressed. Before he would leave, he demanded that Stewart retrieve his metal box of drugs.

"That box was always the first thing the boss thought about. He wouldn't move anywhere without that box," said Stewart.

The other aides had evacuated their families. The little group put Hughes on a stretcher. The quake had knocked out the elevator system and they had to descend by the stairwell. The stairwell was used by the hotel for storage and the passage was clogged with a jumble of spare mattresses. Two of the aides went ahead and cleared a path.

The Hughes party had two Mercedes in the parking lot. They put Hughes in the back seat of one of them and Stewart with him, and drove to an adjoining baseball field. Aftershocks from the quake were still shaking the hotel and they parked in the open so the hotel wouldn't crash down on them if it collapsed.

When the quake waned, Stewart went back into the hotel and retrieved a pillow and a blanket for Hughes. As soon as he was made comfortable, he went to sleep.

The sun rose on a scene of devastation and chaos. More than 5,000 had died and two thirds of the capital city's 325,000 population were homeless. Near the Lake Managua shorefront, the earth had split open and swallowed buildings, automobiles, people. Fires raced unchecked through the rubble. The water system was shattered and the communication lines were down. The area around the hotel was swarming with soldiers, patrolling against looters.

At Hughes's suggestion, Eckersley, Stewart, and the billionaire rode around the ruined city futilely trying to locate an electric generator. "I don't know what we would have done with it if we had found one," Stewart said.

"The boss was upset about the smoke and dust arising from the rubble. He kept saying, 'You can't go down that street.' After a while someone got in touch with Somoza, and he suggested that we take Mr. Hughes out to a country place he had, with a swimming pool."

Eckersley dropped off Hughes and Stewart at the Somoza house, where Stewart secluded the billionaire in a large cabana alongside the pool. Eckersley went back into the ruined city to try to find out what could be done, and Stewart was left alone to guard the billionaire.

"He complained that the light was too bright, and I rigged the blanket across the windows to protect his eyes," Stewart said. "He was afraid also that some of the soldiers at Somoza's place would come and look in at him. I was using my pocket knife to fix up the blanket at the window. In my hurry it slipped and I cut my thumb open; I still have the scar."

Hughes seemed strangely aloof from the devastation around him. "He never asked once about the death toll," Stewart said. "At one point he did say some funds should be sent down from his organization to help rebuild the hospitals. Later I was told that Bill Gay vetoed the idea of giving Nicaragua any money.

"While I was taking care of him at Somoza's place he told me, 'Mell, I know now who my friends are. You have extended yourself well beyond the call of duty.' Then he asked me how much I was being paid. When I told him he seemed upset. He said he wanted my salary raised to the same level as the other aides. But when we got out of the earthquake, nothing was ever said or done about it."

One of the aides got out of the Managua airport on a plane to Guatemala City and sent an urgent message to Romaine to send in an executive jet. Another aide arranged for the families of the Hughes party to fly out to the United States on an Air Force cargo plane.

When the jet arrived to evacuate Hughes, a bitter argument broke out at the airport. Almost all the available space on the jet was crowded with the files and equipment they were taking with them.

"Hughes didn't want to take Fred Jayka and another assistant named John Peterson because they had never seen him," Stewart said. "He was going to leave them behind in that wrecked city.

"Jim Rickard put his foot down. It was one of the few times anyone really spoke up openly against the boss. Rickard said there was *no way* they were leaving the two guys behind. And you know what? The boss backed down."

The party took off, exhausted, tense, and with no firm plans about their final destination. They flew back to Fort Lauderdale to reconnoiter. Hughes stayed aboard the plane while aides shuttled in and out for telephone calls to Romaine and to Chester Davis.

"Hughes was adamant about not remaining in Florida," Stewart said. "He said there would be all kinds of problems about subpoenas and litigation."

Hughes finally agreed to a short stayover in Florida, and was taken off to seclusion. Francom and Stewart were given permission to fly home to Utah to spend the Christmas holidays with their families.

"I flew in, got home very late, kissed my wife hello, and fell into bed," Stewart said. "I was home just seven hours. The next morning, while opening the Christmas presents, I got a call from Romaine. They told me I was going to London and that I had to get my tail back down to Florida. There were times when serving Hughes was a great deal like being in the army.

"Instead of spending Christmas with my family, I spent it on a series of planes. I made a connection in St. Louis, and arrived back in Florida just twenty-four hours after I had left Florida. We loaded Hughes on a plane shortly after I got there and took off for London. We refueled in upstate New York, Newfoundland, and Ireland. By the time we got to London, all the arrangements had been made and we took Mr. Hughes to the Inn on the Park, a hotel owned by the Rothschilds. When we had him tucked safely away, I fell into bed and slept for forty-eight hours."

Margulis fared somewhat better. He was on home leave and got to spend Christmas day with Pat and his young son. He received his unexpected off-to-London orders the day after Christmas. He flew over to

Los Angeles to catch the plane to London and was met by a courier from Romaine.

The courier gave Margulis eighteen checks for baggage that already had been loaded aboard the plane. The messengers didn't know where Hughes would be tucked away in London, but someone would meet Margulis at the airport there with instructions.

"They couldn't tell me *who* would meet me, because the whole move to London had been thrown together in a scramble," Margulis said. "So I came into the London airport with this big pile of baggage and boxes. I had enough luggage to make Elizabeth Taylor look like a piker.

"The customs man looked at the pile and he looked at me. He asked me if all that stuff were mine. I had to say yes because we were never supposed to mention Mr. Hughes's name. He asked me what was in it, and I was stuck. I had to tell him I didn't know. I didn't know whether it was files for the boss, or a new supply of movies, or maybe just a replacement shipment of paper towels and Kleenex for his insulation, or all three."

The airport officials got suspicious. Margulis had a British passport and it showed that he had been bouncing in and out of a lot of countries while listing his residence in Las Vegas. In England some people think of mobsters when they think of Las Vegas.

"They asked me where I was going in London, and I had to tell them I didn't know," Margulis related. "I said that I was waiting for a chap who would tell me where to go. They asked me who this chap might be, and I had to say that I didn't know. Then they went off into a huddle, and a security man came over and asked me if I would submit to a search. They figured that they had some international Mafia courier on their hands. I told them to go ahead and they patted me down to make sure I wasn't armed. It was too bad I couldn't tell them I worked for Howard Hughes. That would have explained everything."

About that time a breathless courier arrived and shepherded Margulis and the luggage through customs.

"He told me that everyone was at the Inn on the Park," Margulis said. "But the chap didn't know what rooms the Hughes party had. When we got to the hotel, I knew I couldn't ask for the Hughes group because they never registered that way. So I asked the desk man for Allen Stroud.

"The chap consulted his records. 'I'm sorry, sir,' he told me, 'but we do not have a Mr. Stroud registered here.'

"Just then I looked around and who did I see? Allen Stroud. I told him I was very happy to see him.

"For all their money and manpower," said Margulis, "there were times when the Hughes organization was not what you would call a model of flawless efficiency."

[12]
THE SIXTY-SEVEN-YEAR-OLD AIRMAN

The stay in London began auspiciously. Two weeks after Hughes settled in at the Inn on the Park, the Supreme Court handed down its decision in TWA *vs.* Hughes. By a six-to-two majority, the court reversed all the lower findings in the marathon case and found that Hughes had no culpability in his management of Trans World Airlines. The judgment against him, now in excess of $170 million with accumulated interest, was thrown out.

British reporters converged on the Inn to record the reaction of the billionaire to the news that he was suddenly $170,000,000 richer than he thought he was. An aide was authorized to inform them that Mr. Hughes "was absolutely ecstatic."

And so, with cause, was Attorney Chester Davis. Twelve years of litigating the case had made him a wealthy man, but there is more to life than money. His legal insights into the complex case were now vindicated. For Chester Davis, it was a Walter Mitty daydream. The decision of the Supreme Court swung on the point he had raised at the very beginning of the case—that Hughes was immune from any antitrust suit because his management of the airline had the approval of the federal Civil Aeronautics Board. On that red-letter day of January 10, 1973, the highest court in the United States turned twelve years of bitter and unbroken defeat for Chester Davis into sweet triumph.

It was not, however, the U.S. judicial system's finest hour. The final decision of the Supreme Court held, in effect, that for twelve years the lower courts had gone the wrong way and had ignored the pivotal point in the case. In his dissenting opinion, Chief Justice Warren Burger expressed his dismay that it had taken so much time and such huge sums of money to reach a conclusion that could have been reached years earlier.

"To describe this litigation as the twentieth-century sequel to *Bleak House* is only a slight exaggeration," he wrote. "Dickens himself could scarcely have imagined that 56,000 hours of lawyering at a cost of $7,500,000 would represent the visible expenses of only one party to a modern intercorporate conflict, to say nothing of the time of corporate and management personnel diverted from their daily tasks. Indeed, today's ending is quite a surprise—as great a surprise to some of us as it must be for the parties. I suggest it will even surprise the victors, for in the oral argument to this court, only a few fleeting comments were devoted to the point that now becomes the dispositive issue in the case."

In his novel *Bleak House*, Dickens had wryly observed that "the one great principle of British law is to make business for itself."

The $170 million gave Hughes's spirits, already on the upbeat from his cautious little sallies into the outer world, a sensational lift. For years he had been thinking and talking about flying again—taking over the controls of a plane himself—and now he decided to *do* it.

But if he was going to fly, he would have to have some clothes. He could hardly man the controls of a jet wearing his drawstring shorts and an old bathrobe.

Margulis got the assignment of outfitting Hughes for his return to the days of his younger glory. "They picked me, I suppose, because I was a Londoner and knew the proper shops," and Margulis. "So I headed for the proper shop. We went out to Simpson's in the West End, a very expensive establishment. I'd always wanted to buy clothes at Simpson's."

Margulis was accompanied by Jack Real, as a sort of stand-in for Hughes. Real, fortunately, was the same height as Hughes—six feet four—and gave Margulis something to size up his purchases against.

"I bought eight light-blue shirts—four with short sleeves and four with long sleeves—and two suits. I didn't ask the price of anything. I don't know what the salespeople thought. I'd ask Jack, 'Do you like that?' and he'd say OK and I'd say, 'All right, we'll take *that*.'

"After I bought those clothes, Mr. Hughes decided that he wanted the kind of old leather flight jacket that he had worn when he was flying back in the 1930's and 1940's. We went back out and scoured London, and finally found the right kind of leather jacket in a thrift shop.

"Then we discovered that his old snap-brim hat was missing, the one Mell had rustled up for him in Las Vegas. It probably got left behind in Managua during the earthquake. So I had to go out and find a snap-brim Stetson, which wasn't the easiest thing to do in London in 1973. I located some at Dunn's hat shop. We were in luck and they had his size.

"While we were fitting him out, I tried to get him a new supply of drawstring shorts, because he was down to just a couple of pair. If there is any shop in London that carries drawstring shorts, I wasn't able to find it."

The where-do-we-get-drawstring-shorts question was solved internally by the Hughes entourage. Fred Jayka, the functionary Hughes had wanted to leave in Managua, said he was a proficient amateur tailor and would be happy to whip up some underwear for the billionaire. A courier went to a fabric shop and got a few yards of linen. Using one of the old pairs for a pattern, Jayka cut and stitched up some of the mandatory no-button underpants that Hughes required. "Old Fred was quite a sight, sitting at a desk sewing away at the boss's underpants, with his glasses down on his nose," said Stewart. "We started calling him 'granny.' "

With his slightly oversized shirt, a thrift-store jacket, a pair of slacks from Simpson's, some home-made underwear, and a brand-new 1940 vintage Stetson, Howard Hughes was ready to fly again.

He was sixty-seven years old, he hadn't flown for at least twelve years, and his eyesight was so poor he couldn't read without a magnifying glass. His weight was down to around 120 pounds, and he was poorly coordinated.

"He was slow-moving and sometimes when he had been to the bathroom it would take me a good five minutes to get him settled back into bed the way he wanted," said Margulis.

On top of all this, he did not have a valid pilot's license. His medical certificate had expired in the late 1950's. For several years thereafter, rather than risk a turndown by an examining doctor, he had simply flown without one.

No one in his entourage was about to raise any legal objections to the billionaire's plans. None of them, however, was eager to go along with him physically.

"Normally there was considerable elbowing between the aides to get closer to the boss," said Margulis. "But when he insisted he was going to fly, they were elbowing the other way."

Stewart put it bluntly. "Howard Hughes doesn't have enough money to get me on a plane that he's flying."

One of the aides sounded out Margulis.

"I told him that I couldn't go on the flight because it was against my religion."

"What do you mean?" the aide asked. "How could flying be against your religion?"

"I'm an orthodox coward," said Margulis.

Jack Real had a private jet brought in and stationed at Hatchfield airport. Then some problems developed.

Hughes wanted the plane remodeled so that he could be hoisted directly into the cockpit. Real told him that was not feasible.

Real had lined up a young English jet pilot, Tony Blackburn, to fly with Hughes. No one seriously thought that Hughes, at his advanced age and beset with so many infirmities, actually proposed to handle the plane in the takeoff and landings; he could hold down the copilot's seat and take over the controls for a while once Blackburn got the jet airborne.

When this was diplomatically spelled out to the billionaire, he objected strenuously.

"What do you mean, I fly copilot?" he complained. "I've never flown copilot in my life."

Blackburn, a young man with his whole life ahead of him, was adamant. He sent word that Hughes would fly copilot with *him* or they would have to find themselves another pilot. Hughes grumbled but gave in.

Finally one morning Margulis got the order for the chicken sandwiches that meant Hughes was going off on a plane. He made up a packet, along with the mandatory bottle of Poland water, and helped Hughes descend from his hideout down the service elevator to the hotel garage. With his snap-brim hat and his leather jacket, the man who had broken the round-the-world flight record almost forty years earlier boarded an old Daimler limousine and went off to re-live the joys of long-gone days.

With Blackburn firmly in the pilot's seat, Hughes "flew" two or three times. Real went along each time, and two senior aides, John Holmes and Jim Rickard, accompanied the billionaire.

"Poor John wasn't very happy about the honor," said Margulis. "He was the sort of chap who would fasten his seat belt in his car at a drive-in movie. But there had to be some aides along in case of an emergency landing."

There was only one narrow escape, and it occurred on land, not in the air. Someone in the entourage developed a cozy relationship with a London *Daily Mirror* reporter and talked out of turn. On one of the flights a reporter and a photographer picked up the Daimler on its way back to the hotel. The press car pulled alongside and the photographer got a picture, of sorts, of Howard Hughes.

"Jack Real spotted the photographer in the nick of time and put a newspaper over the old man's head," said Margulis. "So the *Daily Mirror* ran a big picture of a man with a newspaper over his head. In more than fifteen years, it was the nearest thing to a picture of the boss that any newsman ever got."

[ ]

In March, Hughes decided that the time had come to resolve the long stalemate with the state of Nevada. For more than two years, the casino reorganization plan had been stalled and the state had kept Chester Davis off the Hughes license. All the efforts of the Hughes empire to bend Governor O'Callaghan to the billionaire's will had failed.

Another message was sent to Bill Gay, who had invited Governor O'Callaghan to Nicaragua. Hughes would grant the Nevada governor and his gambling chairman, Phil Hannafin, a face-to-face meeting in

London. Hughes's message contained an addendum calculated to waltz Bill Gay's spirits up to the mountain top.

When Hughes met with the Nevada officials, Hughes said surprisingly that both Bill Gay and Chester Davis could attend the conference.

Just as no one in Nevada had known, until his dethronement, that Robert Maheu never met face-to-face with Hughes, no one outside the Palace Guard knew that Bill Gay hadn't seen Hughes for more than a decade. And Chester Davis, architect of the twelve-year legal triumph over TWA, had never even laid eyes upon his premier client.

The aides took the news of the upcoming conference with the governor in stride. But the impending arrival of Bill Gay sent a charge of excitement through the entourage. The senior aides showered the lower echelons with a series of directives on how to conduct themselves when the executive put in his appearance. The locally hired outer guards were informed that Mr. Gay was a person of high standing in the organization and was to be treated with proper deference. The functionaries, who tended to lounge about their sealed-off quarters in informal attire, were instructed to shape up and bedeck themselves in suits and neckties. And no horseplay or practical jokes.

"The way the senior aides carried on about Bill Gay," said Mell Stewart, "you would have thought we were being visited by the Pope."

Their deference to Gay was a tribute to the power he had accumulated over the years. Both Margulis and Stewart had quietly observed the process from inside the Hughes enclave. Phone messages and memoranda from Gay always went directly in to the billionaire. Information from other segments of the empire were held up pending a telephone call to the Summa center. Unfavorable information and news was cut off at the pass, and Hughes was constantly fed information that put Gay in a good light.

"The aides even told the boss that Gay was such a genius at casino operation that the other casino operators up and down the Las Vegas strip used to confer with him once a month to seek his advice," said Margulis. "When I was back in Vegas on a visit, I checked up on that story. I know a lot of casino people there. They just shook their heads and laughed."

Stewart kept bumping against the same control of information. Stewart was Hughes's personal male nurse, and the billionaire was reluctant to grant Stewart the customary two-weeks-on and two-weeks-off work schedule he permitted the other aides. To pacify Stewart, Hughes told him he could bring his wife and family to London at the billionaire's expense.

"But when I applied for the expense money, the senior aides told me the boss had changed his mind," Stewart said. "When I talked to him again, I found out this wasn't true. They finally doled out enough money so my family had a two-week trip to London. They were sore at me for tripping them up.

"My job was to take care of Mr. Hughes, not to fawn over Bill Gay," said Stewart. "When he showed up in London and came up to the suite, the guard snapped to like one of those fellows at Buckingham Palace when the queen showed up. I was sitting there in a bathrobe with my feet propped up, eating some lamb chops. I looked up at Gay and waved a lamb chop and said, "Hi, coach!" It almost broke the guard up."

The meeting with the governor took place on the eve of St. Patrick's Day. The governor flew in during the morning with Hannafin, registered at another hotel, and went over to the Inn on the Park after midnight.

Hughes, accompanied by Gay and Davis and three aides, Myler, Francom, and Rickard, received the two Nevada officials clad in a bathrobe. He used a hearing aid and after a few pleasantries got down to business and the session lasted slightly more than an hour. Again, he shook hands with his visitors both at the beginning and the close of the conference.

When word of this leaked out, it again prompted skeptics to insist that the Hughes entourage had staged a charade for the Nevadans with the use of a double.

"That's rubbish," said Margulis, and Stewart agreed. "To our knowledge there was never any double used for the boss in his last ten years."

The man the Nevadans saw was neatly groomed and barbered. After the meeting the governor consistently refused to discuss Hughes's condition on the record with any reporters, and he turned down proposals that he write a firsthand account of his encounter with the ghostliest of all Nevada casino owners. But he privately discounted the stories of Hughes's bizarre appearance. He had no way of knowing that the meeting was held up until after midnight because Mell Stewart had spent hours cutting Hughes's hair and beard, and trimming his nails.

The encounter between O'Callaghan and Davis had a touchy background. Davis had offended the governor, during the Maheu ouster, by berating the newly elected O'Callaghan's close friend, political protégé, and lieutenant governor, Harry Reid. "That man's a bully," O'Callaghan had told his friends, "and I don't like bullies." However, one of those present during the conference with Hughes noted, "Davis was as meek as a puppy."

Hughes confirmed to O'Callaghan and Hannafin that he approved the casino license changes, including the nomination of Chester Davis. That was all that Governor O'Callaghan had wanted to know and the next morning he and Hannafin flew home to Nevada.

Twenty-seven months after the casino issue had arisen, it was finally settled. Hughes was always a notorious procrastinator, but what had held up the licensing of Chester Davis for more than two years was not Hughes's indecision.

The issue was whether the elected governor or the economic clout of the Hughes empire was the superior power in the state of Nevada. What is remarkable, in retrospect, was that such a conflict had ever been posed.

[ ]

Bill Gay came to London with a proposal for Hughes. For months he had had designers and architects at work on an elaborate Las Vegas project that he had conceived himself. It had the scope and imagination that he felt would appeal to the billionaire. It was an elaborate Fashion Center that would occupy the stretch of the Las Vegas Strip between the two key Hughes hotels, the Desert Inn and the Sands.

Gay's Fashion Center had been designed by a new Hughes division that Gay recently had brought into being. It was called Archi-System, and consisted of city planners, architects, draftsmen—an integrated team capable of taking on large-scale urban development projects. It had a top-flight staff, including Mrs. Otis Chandler, the wife of the publisher of the Los Angeles *Times*, who had taken courses in city planning. It was a group with considerable talent, but so far few commissions. Gay had put it to work constructing an elaborate mock-up of his Las Vegas Fashion Center so that Hughes could see in miniature Bill Gay's vision for Las Vegas.

Like Chester Davis, who persevered through twelve years of legal setbacks, Gay had daydreams of a comeback himself. In the 1960's he had conceived and headed up a Hughes division called Hughes Dynamics, an ambitious venture into the expanding computer industry. It hadn't got off the ground, although it progressed to the point that Gay had installed elaborate offices in the Kirkeby Center in Westwood. The offices were equipped with carpeting so thick that it had to be hoisted up the building in a helicopter and shoved in through a window.

Bob Maheu asserted later that Hughes was not even aware of Hughes Dynamics until it had gone $8 million into the red. "Hughes heard about it from Jean Peters," Maheu said. "One day she had lunch in the Kirkeby Center and the captain told her he was pleased that her husband had opened such a fine new office in the building. She went home and told Hughes. He took a look at the balance sheet and said, 'Close it down.' "

Others in the Hughes empire confirm Maheu's account. They add that the collapse of Hughes Dynamics was at least a factor in the sudden rise of Robert Maheu when Hughes shortly afterwards moved to Las Vegas.

But that was past unpleasant history. Gay had survived and was now intent upon erasing an old failure with a bright new success.

The mock-up was uncrated and erected in The Office. When it was properly in place, Hughes was briefed on the project.

Hughes said he didn't want any Fashion Center in Las Vegas. The aides suggested that he take a look at the miniature out in The Office. Hughes said he didn't want to look at the mock-up, because he didn't want a fashion center.

"They kept after him for quite some time," said Mell Stewart, "until he finally blew up. He had a real temper when he was pushed too far. I was there when he cut loose.

"He said, 'I told you once, and I'll tell you one more time. I don't *want* a fucking fashion center and I don't want it ever raised again. I want you to tell Gay that that project is dead, dead, dead.'

"The aides went out and covered the mock-up with sheets," Stewart said. "Hughes said, 'They're driving me crazy with that fashion center.'

"When we left London, the mock-up was still sitting out in The Office covered with sheets. The boss didn't even glance at it when they carried him out."

During Hughes's year in London the Rolls-Royce Company encountered severe financial difficulties. The company's troubles arose out of its venture into jet-engine manufacturing for planes and the red ink threatened to engulf its prestigious Rolls-Royce and Bentley autos—long the standards of excellence for the automotive world.

Hughes was dismayed when he learned this. In his younger days he had been an automobile buff, and he had once blown $500,000 in an unsuccessful attempt to construct a steam-powered car that would outperform the Stanley Steamer. In his later years he had acquired his well-known addiction to nondescript Chevies, but this was because no one paid attention to nondescript Chevrolets and hence they accommodated his secrecy fetish.

Several times he told Margulis that he thought he would explore the possibility of helping the Rolls-Royce firm out of its financial woes. "It would be a shame for that fine car to disappear," he said. Like so many of his plans in his latter years, this one too went nowhere, and the Rolls-Royce survived without his help.

He also contemplated a huge infusement of money into the Lockheed plane manufacturing company, which had financial problems that threatened its existence. Hughes discussed this a number of times with Jack Real, the former Lockheed vice-president who was now in the entourage. At one point a story leaked out to the press that Hughes was going to help Lockheed out of its financial morass.

"The aides didn't like that at all," said Margulis. "If the boss was going to splash money around, they wanted it to go into Gay's Fashion Center."

There were a number of instances, Stewart and Margulis said, when Hughes would tell the senior aides that he wanted to talk to Real. "They would go out for a while and then come back and tell Hughes that Real wasn't around and they couldn't locate him. This happened when Real was in his room, waiting to talk to Hughes."

"The collusion around Hughes was so thick you could cut it with a dull knife," said Stewart.

Lockheed, like Rolls-Royce, survived, rescued by a massive money transfusion from the federal government.

Hughes's compassion for things—like Rolls-Royce cars and Lockheed planes—as opposed to people, such as the victims of the Nicaragua earthquake, reflected a self-appraisal Hughes made back in his middle years. One of the last writers he talked to before disappearing into seclusion was Dwight Whitney, a Los Angeles magazine writer.

Hughes described his father as "plenty tough" but a man with a "hail-fellow-well-met quality that I never had. He was a terrifically loved man. I am not. I don't have the ability to win people the way he did.

"I suppose I'm not like other men. Most of them like to study people. I'm not nearly as interested in people as I should be, I guess. What I am interested in is science, nature in its various manifestations, the earth and the minerals that come out of it."

Everyone in the party, including Hughes, liked London. The press was not aggressive, and the staff was able to relax, although the conventional security precautions were observed. Vince Kelley, a former Los Angeles police officer and the Romaine electronics expert, was flown to London and installed a closed-circuit TV system to monitor the back stairwell and the elevator landing.

There was only one security incident. It turned out to be a comedy of errors, like the laundry-bag "bomb" in Vancouver. Some English sporting gentleman, on the floor below the Hughes party, brought in a couple of pheasants he had shot and made the mistake of hanging them out on his balcony. The next morning they were gone. An alert Hughes guard spotted the bag they were in, and taking no chances, rigged a device and reached down and cut the bag free. Some unknown London pedestrian, courtesy of the Hughes party, got a free pheasant dinner.

The Inn on the Park had one drawback. A number of the aides and doctors were ardent tennis fans. At the resort hotels in the past, getting on a court was no problem, but the Inn had no tennis courts. One of the aides discovered that there was a posh private club nearby, the Queen's Tennis Club.

He called up and said that he and his friends would like to join. Informed that it was a *private* club, he said, "We're with the Hughes party at the Inn on the Park, and the expense is no problem." A frosty British voice informed him that at the Queen's Tennis Club the possession of sufficient money to pay its dues was not a criterion for membership.

The happy London days, begun so brightly with Hughes's $170,000,000 windfall, plunged into disaster in the early summer.

While being helped to the bathroom by Levar Myler, Hughes lost his footing and fell. With little flesh to cushion his emaciated frame, he broke the femur in his right hip when he crashed to the floor. A London radiologist was summoned to the Inn, and verified the fracture. Hughes insisted that he wanted the break treated at the Hotel. An approach was made to Dr. Walter Robinson of London, a distinguished orthopedic surgeon, who was asked to perform the operation at the Inn on the Park. The doctor was told that an operating room would be set up at the hotel, fully equipped, and that expense would be no object.

Dr. Robinson refused to perform the remedial work anywhere except in a hospital. "I will not perform such a procedure in a hotel room," the surgeon told a Hughes aide, "and the size of the fee has nothing to do with my decision." Arrangements were therefore made at the London Clinic, where Dr. Robinson preferred to operate. Hughes was booked into the clinic under the name "Hugh Winston."

Margulis and Howard Eckersley handled the transfer of the billionaire to the clinic. Whenever he had to be lifted, Hughes insisted that the muscular Margulis handle him. He was taken down from the Inn on a stretcher and loaded into a little English-built minibus.

"He was very stoic about it, and he had to be in considerable pain," said Margulis. "It was the little troubles that seemed to bother him, not the big ones. When we got him settled in the little van, he looked around and said, 'This is a nice little bus and we ought to buy one like it and keep it on hand.'"

"He had had another fall, back in Nassau," Stewart recalled. "I was with him one day and he went into the bathroom. All of a sudden I heard this noise and rushed in and there was Hughes, lying naked under the sink looking up at me piteously. 'Get me out of here, Mell,' Hughes told me, 'I think I've busted my tit.' I helped him into the bed and told him I'd better call a doctor. He said he'd wait awhile and see how he felt the next day. He *hated* to have doctors poke around him. A couple of days later Dr. Chaffin finally looked him over and found that he was just bruised."

Dr. Thain took a room at the London clinic and stayed on stand-by during the operation. It took several hours for Dr. Robinson to set the fracture and secure the break with a metal surgical pin.

"I was up in Hughes's room a couple of days later and a nurse came in to take some blood for a test," said Margulis. "She went over to his bed and the boss's mind was off somewhere, or else he forgot that he was supposed to be Hugh Winston.

"The nurse said, 'Mr. Winston,' and Hughes didn't pay any attention. She said, 'Mr. Winston!' three times until finally I had to speak up and tell Mr. Hughes that she was talking to *him*.

"When she told him she needed a blood sample, he was very polite and cooperative, which was unusual for him."

Within a few days, however, Hughes demanded that the hospital stay be cut short. "I'm going back to the hotel now," he told his aides, and over the doctor's objections he was spirited back to the Inn on the Park.

In quitting the hospital prematurely, Hughes was repeating a self-injuring act of intransigence that he had committed more than a quarter of a century earlier. In 1946, when he had crashed an experimental reconnaisance plane of his own design in Beverly Hills, he had been pulled from the flaming wreckage badly burned, suffering multiple fractures and barely alive. For a week his life was in the balance, but then he had come out of the crisis. Within a few weeks he announced that he'd had enough of the hospital and ordered his underlings to take him home. His doctors had a whole series of surgical procedures scheduled—including the repair of a smashed cheekbone—and they were appalled at his departure. "I don't know how he got out of the hospital," one of them said at the time. "He must have flown his hospital bed out of the place."

He had lived on with a caved-in cheek and internal injuries and displacements that time and proper surgery could have repaired or relieved.

His kidney trouble had begun shortly afterwards. His internal disarray also had aggravated a chronic case of constipation that had plagued him from his youth. From then on until his death, most of his waking hours were taken up with these dual eliminative problems. For more than twenty-five years, he had been dependent upon periodic colonic irrigation to rid his system of waste. He aggravated the problem with his bizarre eating habits and with his penchant for procrastination; once in London he went twenty-eight days in a state of constipation.

But again in London, as in Southern California, no one would interpose his will against that of Hughes, no matter how urgent or sensible such an interposition might be. With those who served him, to hear was to obey.

"We took him back into the Inn through the loading dock," Margulis said. "The big problem that everyone was concerned with was not that he was leaving the clinic too soon, but getting him back to the Inn without anyone seeing him.

"I guarded a doorway from the hotel while the aides moved him onto the service elevator. I almost got into a knockdown with two workmen leaving the hotel. I told them they couldn't go out that door and we got into a pushing contest. I held them off until they got the boss on the elevator. Then I went on up and helped lift him into his bed.

"From then on, it was all downhill for the boss. For the final two and a half years of his life, he never walked again."

In December the entourage got word that Hughes was returning to the Bahamas. The aides and functionaries who had gone through the ordeal at the Britannia Beach Hotel in Nassau were dismayed and outraged at the news.

"I just couldn't understand why we were deliberately going back into that bear trap, after we had all that trouble getting out of there," said Stewart.

"It made no sense," said Margulis, "and even the senior aides, who always took orders and asked no questions, were upset. It was almost as if we were looking for trouble."

271

No one bothered to explain the reasons for the move. The members of the entourage were simply told to pack up and go.

On the flight out of London, after the plane had been airborne a few hours, Hughes asked Margulis to "put something up so everyone can't be looking at me all the time." The "everyone" meant the immediate members of his inner circle. Margulis got a blanket, tied some cord to the corners, and strung it up across the middle of the plane.

"That's better," said Hughes. "Have you got any magazines, Gordon?"

"Nothing you'd be interested in," said Margulis, handing him *Ring*, a magazine on boxing, and a magazine on the art of karate.

The karate magazine interested Hughes and he studied it carefully. "This is interesting stuff," said the frail old man. "You mean to say you work on this when you're off duty?"

Margulis told him that he studied karate under Saul Tallbear, a Mohawk Indian expert in Las Vegas. He and Hughes had a long discussion about the Oriental art of self-defense.

At one point, George Francom stuck his head over the curtain to check up on his employer. Hughes seemed upset.

"Did you hear what we were talking about, George?" Hughes asked.

Francom shook his head and went back to his seat.

"We'll have to talk about this some more," said Hughes. "But don't tell any of the others."

His small ventures out into life were ended, and he

was headed back down into even darker isolation. Now he was hiding trivial small talk from his closest aides. Gordon promised faithfully that he would tell no one about Hughes and karate. Hughes never brought the subject up again.

[13]
SANCTUARY

It was the sixth move for the traveling asylum in three years, but this time it looked as if the restless wandering had come to an end. The party flew to Freeport on Grand Bahama Island, north up the island chain from Nassau. They settled in at the Xanadu Princess Hotel, owned by the wealthy shipping magnate Daniel K. Ludwig. Shortly afterward the Hughes organization bought the hotel outright, and it appeared that the billionaire at long last had found a permanent home-away-from-home.

Whoever had handled the advance arrangements for the return to the Bahamas had done their work well. The hostility that had touched off the flight in 1972 had vanished. The government had undergone a sea change, and the political climate was as warm and friendly as the tropical breezes that wafted off the Gulf Stream.

Hughes urgently needed a friendly and protective sanctuary. He had come under criminal indictment in federal court in Nevada on charges of fraudulent stock manipulation in his acquisition of Air West. Unlike a civil suit, in which he could be represented in court by his attorneys, a criminal case required his personal appearance. If he failed to show up for his arraignment, he could be declared a fugitive from justice. Apart from the public relations nightmare that this would pose, he would also be vulnerable to legal sanctions that could damage his empire.

Hughes now was totally immobile. He had to be carried to the bathroom and carried back, and those were the only times he stirred from his bed. Dr. Chaffin, Stewart, and Margulis took turns trying to convince him that he should follow the series of exercises prescribed by Dr. Robinson in London, but he either stubbornly refused or procrastinated.

"Dr. Chaffin really put the pressure on him to help himself," said Margulis. "He told him that Katharine Hepburn had a hip fracture like his and had followed the proper exercises and was up and walking within months. She was close to Hughes's age, and Hughes had admired her greatly back in the old Hollywood days.

"Hughes would say maybe he'd get started in a few days, but then nothing would happen."

Meanwhile, his platoons of lawyers were energetically working to kill the charges against him in the Air West case. A federal judge in Nevada threw out the indictment once on the grounds that it was improperly drawn. The U.S. attorney in Las Vegas, Devoe Heaton, promptly announced that the grand jury would be reassembled and a new indictment would be drawn. Heaton was then summoned to Washington and advised by his superiors in the Justice Department that Hughes was not a proper target for a new indictment. When word of this leaked out, a news team from *The New York Times* descended on the Justice Department, seeking evidence of political favoritism. The Justice Department denied that any pressure had been put on it by the Nixon administration, and Heaton proceeded to re-indict Hughes. The second indictment was then thrown out, but the case against Hughes was later filed as a civil action by the Securities and Exchange Commission in federal court in San Francisco.

No one outside the Hughes inner circle knew the billionaire's desperate plight. Until the fall in London, his hiding had been a matter of choice and the pressure of his phobias. But now he had retreated deeply into invalidism and was physically, as well as psychologically, incapable of any public appearance.

Fortunately for his attorneys, the Bahamas were a sanctuary from which a person charged with stock fraud could not be deported. Only a month or so before Hughes was moved to the Bahamas, a local magistrate had ruled that the extradition treaty between the islands and the United States, which dated back many years, was no longer binding upon the Bahamas. This ruling had been handed down in favor of Robert Vesco, the financial manipulator who had fled the United States bearing a huge fortune from the wreckage of Bernie *(Do You Sincerely Want to Become Rich)* Cornfeld's overseas investment fiasco. Vesco was under indictment on massive fraud charges in the States, but the magistrate's ruling had sent him smiling from the court.

The New York Times's Hughes expert, Wallace Turner, took notice of the series of events: the indictment of Hughes, the "Vesco decision" establishing the Bahamas as a sanctuary from deportation, the sudden and unexpected return of Hughes to the Bahamas. Hughes's publicist Hannah expressed outrage at the notion that the billionaire had ducked down to a country where he would be beyond the reach of United States law. But he offered no explanation as to why the billionaire had returned to the locale of his nightmare flight.

Early in September the U.S. consul in Nassau, Marvin Groeneweg, received a court summons for Hughes in the Air West case and flew up to Freeport to serve it. When he inquired for Hughes at the Xanadu Princess Hotel, which Hughes now owned, he was given the standard evasion that the management knew nothing about any Howard R. Hughes. Since Hughes's arrival there had been widely publicized, Groeneweg persisted. He consulted the Freeport postmaster and was told that the Hughes organization had authorized a Bahamian Hughes employe, Vance Tynes, to accept mail for Hughes. Groeneweg looked up Tynes and handed him the summons.

The following week Groeneweg had an indignant visit from Robert Peloquin, Washington attorney, former U.S. Justice Department official, and now president of Intertel, the high-priced private intelligence operation that had Hughes as a client. Peloquin told the U.S. consul that the summons had been improperly served and that he would need to hand the document to Hughes in person to have it honored.

Groeneweg said he would be willing to do so, and asked Peloquin how he could arrange to meet Hughes. According to an affidavit the consul later executed, Peloquin told him that "any consular officer would find Mr. Hughes quite inaccessible." With Hughes protected by the "Vesco decision," the sovereign U.S. government had no alternative but to accept this somewhat imperial rebuff.

Although its proprietor was a bedridden invalid, the Hughes empire was alive and well and humming with activity. There were daily decisions to be made, and far out in California the Gay-Henley-Davis triumvirate made them. They did not always consult Hughes, and some of their decisions were withheld from him.

With the sale of the Houston tool-bit division, Gay's position became enhanced. Raymond Holliday, executive vice-president of the old Hughes Tool Co. and a veteran power sachem in the empire, left Hughes's employ and went with the spun-off, publicly owned tool-bit company. Bill Gay then became executive vice-president of the new parent company, Summa. He now held formally the Numero Uno position that, for all practical purposes, he had occupied since the toppling of Bob Maheu.

The legendary Romaine Street "operations center" was phased down to little more than a shell. The headquarters for Summa were moved out into the San Fernando Valley, more convenient to Bill Gay, who lived there. The executive offices were installed in three floors of an office building at 17,000 Ventura Boulevard in Encino. All the top officials, including

Gay, Nadine Henley, Kay Glenn, and Robert Bennett took up quarters there.

Hughes, however, had wanted the Summa headquarters centered in Las Vegas, where the most active segments of his empire were located. Although offices for Summa were installed in Las Vegas, the nerve center was in the three floors of a building 300 miles away in Encino.

Oddly, the Encino Summa headquarters for the Hughes empire had no listed telephone number, although it was lavishly equipped with telephones. But there were three listings for Summa in the Las Vegas telephone book, and a direct tie-line between the Las Vegas offices and the Encino headquarters. Anyone calling the Las Vegas Summa offices and seeking Bill Gay or Nadine Henley could be connected directly with the Encino headquarters.

One day at the Xanadu Princess Hotel, senior aide George Francom took a memorandum in to the bedridden billionaire. Gordon Margulis was present. Hughes adjusted his "peepstone," read it, and asked querulously:

"What the hell is this Summa office at 17,000 Ventura Boulevard in Encino?"

Francom told him that it was the headquarters for his holding company.

"Hughes went up in smoke," said Margulis. "He said, 'I told Gay that I wanted everything centered in Las Vegas. What the hell is going on here, anyway? An office in Encino gives us tax problems in California. I'm going to get on the phone to Mickey West and get to the bottom of this.'

"Francom went out into the office," Margulis said,

279

"and told one of the other aides what had happened. Everyone got upset, and they decided Francom would have to be the fall guy.

"Another aide went into Hughes's bedroom and told him that Francom had made a mistake. He said that George was mixed up, and that there wasn't anything in Encino except a small branch installation. He said, 'It's nothing important, Mr. Hughes—just two little offices over a barbershop.'

"The boss calmed down. 'Well, that's all right,' he told the aide, and then he dropped the matter."

Stripping the Romaine center down to a caretaker staff had other and more far-reaching consequences, arising from the entwinement of the Hughes empire with the affairs of the U.S. government. By a convoluted series of farcical events, the cutback in the Romaine staff wound up blowing the cover on one of the CIA's most closely guarded secrets, the mission of the Hughes Glomar Explorer.

The Glomar Explorer was unveiled in 1973 as a daring venture by the Hughes organization into a new frontier—mining valuable minerals such as manganese nodules from the ocean floor. The *Glomar*, a huge, ungainly vessel with an Eiffel Tower–like derrick amidships, was constructed at a York, Pennsylvania, shipyard and sailed around South America to California because it was too big to pass through the Panama Canal. A companion vessel, the HMB-1—for "Hughes Marine Barge"—was built at a California shipyard. The barge was even more odd-looking than the *Glomar*. It was longer than a football field and resembled a seagoing dirigible hangar. The barge had a retractible roof and was submersible, like a submarine.

The purpose of these two vessels, the public was told, was to suck up mineral nodules from the ocean floor with a kind of giant vacuum sweeper installed on the *Glomar* and process them aboard the marine barge. The Hughes organization thus was pictured as risking huge sums of the billionaire's private capital to secure new sources of scarce minerals for the nation's industries.

Actually, Hughes did not invest a penny in the *Glomar*; it served as a cover for a secret CIA project —code name Project Jennifer—that might have brought a smile to the face of Ian Fleming's Dr. No. The *Glomar* was built to salvage a sunken Russian nuclear-armed submarine from three miles down in the Pacific Ocean northwest of Hawaii. The cost of constructing, equipping, and operating the ship and its barge—a staggering $400,000,000, more than twice the cost of the Hoover Dam—was borne entirely by the U.S. taxpayers. Unlike the Hoover Dam, the *Glomar* was financed by the taxpayers without their knowledge. The CIA hoped to fish up the Soviet sub intact and score an intelligence coup by recovering its nuclear missiles and its code books. From the outset, Project Jennifer was encased in the tightest security, comparable to that which concealed the World War II development of the atom bomb. Although some 4,000 construction workers and several hundred crew members and technicians were involved, not a word of the covert mission leaked out in 1974. Early that summer, the *Glomar* rendezvoused with the submersible barge off Catalina Island in Southern California.

The barge carried a giant claw, equipped with underwater lights and remote TV cameras, which was engineered to clamp around the sunken submarine. The barge submerged under the *Glomar* and attached the claw to the vessel, and the *Glomar* then crept off into the Pacific.

There, according to later CIA accounts, the *Glomar* located the sunken sub, clamped its giant claw around it, and began hauling it to the surface. But then something malfunctioned and the major portion of the sub broke loose and fell back to the ocean floor. The *Glomar*—again according to CIA accounts—recovered only one-third of the sub, missing the nuclear missiles and code books. It took this fragment to friendly waters off Hawaii, where the piece was examined by U.S. technicians and later was cut up and jettisoned into the sea. The *Glomar* then returned to the United States for repairs and modifications for a second retrieval attempt aimed at fishing up the rest of the fractured submarine.

This second effort never got under way because early in 1975 the CIA cover story was blown by a series of improbable events. They stemmed from a bizarre burglary that had taken place at the Hughes Romaine Street headquarters eight months earlier.

Shortly after midnight on June 5, 1974, four burglars gained entry to Romaine by overpowering the lone guard on duty, a man named Mike Davis. Trundling a huge acetylene tank and torch on a steel dolly, the burglars went directly up to Kay Glenn's former office on the second floor, where they cut open a Mosler wall vault and looted it. They remained in the building more than four hours, burned open another safe, and ransacked files and desks. When they departed, they left Davis—according to his account—tied up on a couch. Only one other man was on duty in the building, manning the once-busy but now dormant telephone switchboard. He was in a remote, soundproof room and said that he was unaware of the safe-cracking.

The burglary was a one-day story in the press. Newsmen were told that $68,000 in cash, some Wedgwood vases, and a few odds and ends were taken. There were no follow-up accounts and the burglary, seemingly of no great consequence, was soon forgotten.

What newsmen were not told was that the safe-crackers had also obtained two footlockers full of Howard Hughes's confidential memos and documents. Several weeks after the burglary, a man using the name "Chester Brooks" telephoned the Summa headquarters and offered to return the stolen Hughes documents in return for a million dollars in cash. The Summa officials refused to buy them back, on the grounds that the burglars would simply Xerox the confidential papers and return the originals and thus still retain Hughes's secrets. The rebuffed burglars broke off all contact with Summa.

But then, about a month later, Summa officials made a dismaying discovery. They learned that a memorandum outlining Project Jennifer was missing from the Romaine center. The Summa officials concluded that the burglars had made off with the Project Jennifer memo and that one of the nation's top intelligence secrets was in the hands of unknown safe-crackers.

In consternation and embarrassment, Summa informed the CIA of this disaster. It had occurred at a crucial juncture: the *Glomar* was then en route to the Pacific to try to fish up the sunken submarine.

The CIA enlisted the aid of the FBI, in order to conceal its own involvement. The FBI, working through its Los Angeles office, urgently requested Los Angeles Police Chief Ed Davis to try to contact the burglars and retrieve the stolen papers, using a million dollars in federal funds for bait. In order to justify this highly unorthodox police effort, top officials in the Los Angeles Police Department were let in on the *Glomar* secret.

While the police were frantically and unsuccessfully trying to establish communication with the unknown safe-crackers, a Hollywood actor and television scriptwriter named Leo Gordon showed up at the office of the Los Angeles County District Attorney with an electrifying story. He said that he had been approached by a California car salesman named Donald Woolbright. Woolbright had told him that he "had access" to the stolen Hughes documents, Gordon said, and had asked Gordon's help in selling them to some major publication outside the United States. Gordon told the D. A. that he had been shown some of the documents and that they included "politically" explosive information and some references to the CIA.

The District Attorney took Gordon and his story to the Los Angeles police. Delighted at what they believed to be a break in "The Case of the Purloined CIA Secret," they laid elaborate plans to use Leo Gordon and the offer of a million dollars as bait for a trap to get back in touch with the burglars. But no one nibbled on the bait. The end result of the effort to recover the stolen Hughes documents was that details of Project Jennifer became known to too many Los Angeles law enforcement officers.

Early in February, 1975, someone leaked a garbled report of the 1974 sub retrieval to reporter William Farr of the Los Angeles *Times*. The *Times* reported, under a double eight-column banner head on page one, that the *Glomar* had recovered a Russian submarine from the North Atlantic, the wrong ocean and 10,000 miles from the actual recovery. In the following edition, the *Times* moved the story back to page sixteen and then dropped it altogether. In Los Angeles news circles, this inexplicable downplay of a sensational news exclusive became known as "The Case of the Incredibly Shrinking Russian Submarine." Later it developed that the L.A. *Times* had played down and then dropped the story at the urgent request of the CIA, on the grounds that the disclosure was "making waves" with an ongoing major intelligence mission.

Other publications, however, were galvanized into action by the L.A. *Times* story. *New York Times* reporter Seymour Hersh jumped on it and quickly verified and wrote it for publication. The CIA then made a similar appeal to *New York Times* executives and the *Times* likewise held up publication. As other publications nailed down the story, the CIA would confirm it and ask that it be suppressed. Not all newsmen agreed with the suppression of the story; after all, it had been splashed once across the front page of the L.A. *Times* and hence was no secret to any Russian intelligence agent capable of reading English. Finally, columnist Jack Anderson got onto the sub retrieval story and refused to withhold it. The CIA then released the news media from their promises, and the story gushed out in full detail.

After the secret was out, the story took a bizarre turn. The lone guard on duty at Romaine on the night of the burglary, Mike Davis, came forward with some new details. He now said that he had not been totally candid with the police, or with the grand jury that had investigated the burglary and the extortion attempt. In return for a promise that the information would not be used to prosecute him, he now spilled out new facts that he had kept to himself for some ten months.

After the burglars had fled and he had loosened his bonds, Davis said, he had found two documents lying on the floor in Kay Glenn's office, where they presumably had been dropped by the safe-crackers. He had picked them up, he said, and stuffed them in his pocket. One was the Project Jennifer memo, and the other was a bank certificate of deposit for $100,000, made out to Kay Glenn.

Davis said that "in the excitement of the burglary" he had forgotten to tell the police or his employers about his find. He had taken the documents home and squirreled them away, but now he wanted to set things right. And he produced the $100,000 bank certificate for return to its proper owner.

But he could not, unfortunately, return the top-secret Project Jennifer memo, the loss of which had touched off the great security flap and the manhunt for the Romaine burglars. When he had read the newspaper accounts of the sub retrieval project, Davis said, he had panicked, torn up the Project Jennifer memo, and flushed it down his toilet.

Thus all the consternation in Summa and at the CIA had been unnecessary. So had the sharing of the Jennifer secret with the L.A. officials—which had led to the L.A. *Times*'s blowing the cover on the sub project. Everyone had been frantically seeking to retrieve a document that had literally gone down the drain.

This comic-opera denouement went almost unnoticed in the great national controversy over the role of the press in disclosing the CIA's sub retrieval mission. People who disliked the press railed at newsmen for having breached national security. Newsmen uneasy over collaboration between the press and government railed at those editors who had briefly ducked into bed with the CIA and held up the *Glomar* story.

In all this uproar, hardly anyone commented on the cavalier manner in which the Hughes organization had handled the $400 million secret the CIA had entrusted to its care. Police reports, suppressed at the time of the burglary, noted that Romaine had a single burglary alarm system that was not working and hadn't worked for months. Romaine had not been designated as a safe repository for classified information, and its security system—including the use of a single guard—met none of the established federal precautions. Romaine was not even equipped with the standard remote-control TV cameras that the Hughes Secrecy Machine utilized to safeguard the billionaire's personal security. As one detective commented, "Those burglars knocked over Romaine like it was a neighborhood delicatessen."

The Romaine fiasco raised a crucial question that

has not been answered. That was whether the CIA knew the true condition of Hughes when it enlisted his Summa as cover and custodian for a project with grave international implications.

Back in 1971, when Hughes first quit the United States, the editor of the *Armed Forces Journal*, Ben Schemmer, queried the CIA about the security aspects of the billionaire's exiling himself from his country while his organization was involved in highly sensitive defense contracts. Schemmer had asked the CIA if it had assured itself that Hughes was competent, in control of his empire and secure from foreign forces. The CIA responded that it had no jurisdiction over U.S. residents.

There is no evidence and scant reason to believe that the Romaine security breach could be laid to Hughes, who was not even aware that Romaine had been largely abandoned in Bill Gay's move out to Encino. Possibly Hughes was never told of the Romaine burglary. Given his fetish for concealing even the trivia of his life, the loss of two footlockers of his secret papers was a disaster that normally would have sent Hughes into a monumental rage.

But throughout the stay in Freeport neither Margulis nor Stewart heard the billionaire make even a passing reference to the Romaine burglary or the quaint destruction of the Jennifer memo.

[ ]

Having gained the rare privilege of a face-to-face meeting with Hughes in London, Chester Davis came down to Freeport seeking a new audience with his client. Margulis and Stewart soon observed that the arrival of Hughes's chief counsel stirred currents of discontent among the Palace Guard. Davis, they were told, wanted to discuss the senior aides' salaries with Hughes because they posed a problem with the Internal Revenue Service. Their salaries, ranging up to $110,000 a year for Holmes and Myler, were paid by Summa and not by Hughes personally. This relieved the billionaire of any personal tax liability for the aides, and thus put the bulk of the burden of maintaining his personal entourage over on his companies as a business expense.

But with the downfall of Richard Nixon there had been a change of climate in the Internal Revenue Service. IRS agents had belatedly begun asking Bebe Rebozo pointed questions about the tax liability on the $100,000 in Hughes cash that Rebozo had held for over three years without reporting. Rebozo had finally resolved that problem by returning $100,000 to the Hughes organization. Now the IRS was looking at other Hughes expenditures with unwonted curiosity.

"The aides didn't want Davis to talk to the boss," said Margulis. "He was kept sedated for three days while Davis waited to see him. When he finally woke up, he agreed to talk to Davis, but said he wanted to eat first and then have Mell Stewart barber and groom him.

"He took his time eating, as always, but when he was through he told the aides to bring Mell in.

"They went off for a while and came back and told Hughes that they couldn't locate Mell anywhere. It was the same device they used in London, when Hughes would want to talk to Jack Real. I knew Mell was waiting in his room, so I scooted down there and told him to get on up to the boss's bedroom. The aides knew that Davis had to get back to New York, so they kept stalling."

Stewart took his barber tools and went to work on Hughes. "While I was cutting his hair," Stewart said, "I told him that the air crew was waiting and Davis was getting ready to fly out.

"The boss started waving his arms and said, 'You tell Chester not to leave!' So I passed the word to Gordon to tell Davis to hold up. Gordon went down to the tennis court and told Davis that Hughes wanted to see him."

"The aides were mad as hell at both of us," said Margulis. "I told Mell that we had spoiled their little game."

In spite of their efforts, Margulis and Stewart said, Davis never got past the Palace Guard and wound up discussing his business with his client on the telephone.

"When Davis was through," said Margulis, "he called the aides together in Bundy's office and read them the riot act. He said that if he ever heard that they were not passing any of his messages in to Hughes, they were going to be in real trouble."

Stewart said his efforts to keep Hughes in touch with what was going on "put me in the deep freeze."

"Holmes told me, 'God damn it, don't ever volunteer information like that.' From then on, until we left Freeport, I was treated like a traitor and they kept me away from the boss. But my loyalty and obligation was to Mr. Hughes, not to the senior aides or Summa or Bill Gay or Kay Glenn. He was the man I worked for, not any of the others.

"I didn't even see Mr. Hughes until they were putting him on the plane for that last move to Acapulco. He was in bad shape then, but he looked up at me and said, 'Mell, it's nice to see you again.' "

In his last month or so at Freeport, Hughes deteriorated markedly. He began to avoid eating again, and his weight dropped off. "It was as if something had broken his spirit," Margulis said. "He spent days just sleeping, or in a sort of coma. When he was awake, he watched movies but he didn't seem to enjoy them much.

"When we first came down to Freeport, I thought there was a good chance that he would pull himself together, in spite of his broken hip. When we were coming in from the airport, he told me that some people thought he was through but they were wrong.

"He was never a religious man, but he said something I'll always remember. He nodded his head toward the sky and said, 'The Man up there is going to have to wait a little while.' "

Hughes was seventy years old on Christmas Eve of 1975. His birthday, as usual, passed without observance and Christmas day went by the same way.

"One of the aides pulled a little trick that I didn't like at all," said Margulis. "He was on the telephone to the Summa headquarters. I heard him say, 'Mr. Hughes wants to wish Bill Gay and his staff a Merry Christmas and to tell them he appreciates all their work.'

"When he hung up, I told him I didn't think the boss had really said that.

"He just grinned and said he knew, but it would make everyone in Encino feel better."

A little more than a month later, the word was

passed that the entourage was going to move again, this time to Acapulco. By then Hughes was deep into his last steep decline, one that would come to an end on the final flight to Houston.

"When we were told that we were to take the boss to Mexico, I couldn't believe it," said Margulis. "One place was like another to him in that dark little bedroom. When an aide would come on duty, the first question he would ask was whether the boss was 'out of it.' They could have taken him out, repainted the bedroom and then told him that he was in Acapulco and he wouldn't have known the difference."

But on February 12, 1976, the emaciated billionaire was placed in a wheelchair and moved out of the Xanadu Princess and taken in a van to yet another plane. Accompanied by Drs. Chaffin and Crane, Waldron, Holmes, Francom, Real, Stewart, and Margulis, he was flown nonstop across the breadth of the continent and installed in the Acapulco hotel.

When they wheeled him into the elevator at Acapulco, the door malfunctioned. The door would close, but the elevator wouldn't move, and then the door would open again.

"We just stayed there, while the door opened and closed, until finally Hughes became aware something was wrong," said Margulis. "He asked me what the hell was going on.

"I made a little joke. I told him, 'This is your new room. We'll bring your bed in soon, and this is where you're going to live.'

"He caught on in a little while, made his OK signal with his thumb and first finger in a circle, and managed a little smile. It was the last time I ever saw him smile.

"Then the elevator worked and we took him up to his new bedroom. When I carried him in, it was like carrying a frail, long-legged child."

[14]
THE LONE
AND LEVEL SANDS

At the end of *Citizen Kane*, Orson Welles's movie about great wealth and excessive acquisition, the camera pans over a vast hall piled with furniture, statues, suits of armor, and other possessions that Charles Foster Kane—the barely disguised William Randolph Hearst—had gathered unto himself in a long life. In the film, a team from a news magazine had sought and failed to find the explanation for Kane's last word, "Rosebud." As the camera moved over the detritus of Kane's materialism it focused on a little sled that he had preserved from his childhood. A workman, sorting out the things of value, carelessly tosses the sled into a fireplace and the audience sees the name "Rosebud" as the flames consume it. At his death, Kane's mind had gone back to the simple joys of childhood.

On his last day, Howard Hughes was incoherent

and no one understood or preserved his last words. When Margulis lifted him onto the plane to Houston, his lips moved silently but no sound came forth. He died as he had lived, turned inward.

His personal possessions, the things that he owned himself as opposed to his corporate holdings, would have made only a small pile in one corner of his last darkened bedroom. They were scarcely more than those left by Gandhi. For his funeral in Houston, his relatives had to purchase burial clothes—a dark blue suit and all the accessories—for one of the world's richest men.

Like Charles Foster Kane, he left a "Rosebud" unanswered; in fact, two mysteries. One was why he neglected himself, why he turned himself into a man who could not bear to be looked upon. Human aberrations are such that quite possibly Hughes himself did not know what drove him into self-neglect. If he knew the answer, he took this secret with him.

The second "Rosebud" was what he was all about; what he perceived as his goal beyond mere acquisition.

No camera could scan or encompass what Hughes owned and left behind at his death—vast areas of land, companies, hotels, more than $200 million in government notes—but the key to his life was not hidden somewhere in his holdings; they were the mystery itself.

He was the epitome of what the American dream had become in the latter half of the twentieth century —wealth beyond comprehension, the unbridled power implicit in such wealth, the mindless thrust of unleashed technology. His money had fertilized industrial plants that pushed U.S. science into new frontiers, put a camera on the moon, and sent communication satellites orbiting above the world. But he himself could hardly communicate with anyone. In the end the money overwhelmed him and all those who held it in awe; in the end his life funneled down to a small, darkened bedroom where his wealth served no purpose except to buy him the total seclusion that his autistic existence required.

In his telephone interview from the Britannia Beach Hotel, he had expressed a wish to use his wealth for medical research. "Eventually that is where the bulk of my estate will go," he said. "There is nothing that interests me more than medical research and the quest for better living facilities and better health and better medical standards, not only in the United States, but throughout the world."

But he had said many things in that interview, and in other conversations and memos, that he had not meant. He had dangled the promise of his money for medical research in front of Texas, Florida, and Nevada in order to condition politicians so that they would take a compliant attitude toward other things he had wanted.

It would have taken a simple act to bequeath his money to medical research. But when he died a thorough search of his vaults, safety-deposit boxes, and files failed to uncover any will. Had he left his estate to a medical foundation, it would have been to the advantage of Summa officials to produce such a will. The alternative—no will at all—meant that the bulk of his wealth, as much as 75 percent, may go to the federal government in inheritance levies. This will require liquidation of much of his empire, a course that runs counter to the interests of those in power at Summa at his death.

In the flurry of "wills" that turned up after his death, most of them manifestly false, only one was offered for probate. This was the so-called "Mormon will," which was found under mysterious circumstances at the Mormon headquarters in Salt Lake City. It was a handwritten document replete with internal contradictions. Purportedly written in 1968, it named as executor Noah Dietrich, toward whom Hughes harbored deep resentment, a resentment he had expressed in his 1972 interview. The will bequeathed "the Spruce Goose"—a flippant nickname that Hughes detested—to Long Beach, at a time when the federal government, not Hughes, had sole title to the flying boat. The language and style of the will lacked Hughes's precision and concern for detail; it clashed harshly with the meticulosity of his memo on Jane Russell's wardrobe.

The oddest item in the document was the bequest of one-sixteenth of his wealth to Melvin Dummar, a Utah gas-station operator. Dummar claimed to have picked up Hughes on a roadside in 1968 and to have driven him to Las Vegas, where "Hughes" asked to be dropped off at the Sands Hotel and borrowed 25 cents. If Hughes left his Desert Inn suite at any time between 1966 and 1970, his absence went unnoticed by his Palace Guard. Finally, the story of people picking up an indigent who turned out to be Howard Hughes—and rewarded them handsomely—was one of the most persistent folk tales in the Hughesiana.

His final legacy to the world may be simply a long tangle of litigation. Both Margulis and Stewart believe he died without a will. "He used hints of putting some-one in, or cutting them out of his will to keep people in line," said Margulis. "If he had written a will and turned it over to an aide, he would have lost this power. I can see him, when he faced up to death, just saying, 'Screw them all.'"

At the end there was no one for whom he expressed concern except Jean Peters, and he had provided for her in their divorce settlement. He had not seen his closest relative, an aunt, for some forty years, and his other heirs were distant cousins, most of whom had never even met him. His late uncle, the writer Rupert Hughes, graphically described Hughes's relationship with his relatives. "I can get in touch with the Almighty by dropping to my knees," he said, "but I don't know how to reach Howard."

[ ]

He was buried two days after his death, at Glen-wood Cemetery in Houston, next to the graves of his mother and father. It was a private ceremony with sixteen mourners, mainly distant relatives, and no one wept. The Reverend Robert Gibson, of Christ Church Episcopal Cathedral, where Hughes had been baptized as an infant, conducted the brief burial service, which included the passage from the Book of Common Prayer, "We brought nothing into this world and it is certain we can carry nothing out."

None of the top officials of Summa were present. They had not been asked to attend.

Several months later, at a board meeting in Las Vegas, Frank William Gay was elevated to the presidency of Summa Corporation. It was a position that Howard Hughes himself had never held.

Robert Maheu was on a cruise with friends in the Aegean Sea when Hughes died. He heard of the death in a radiogram, and the following day went ashore on the Island of Crete, where he read a newspaper account of the billionaire's death. Two years had passed since a jury had awarded him $2,800,000 in damages because Hughes had falsely branded him a thief, but the Hughes lawyers had appealed and he had not been recompensed.

When he read of Hughes's sad final state, he wept. His wife, Yve, asked him why.

"No one deserves to go the way he went," said Maheu.

Out in Las Vegas, where the Hughes resorts rise from the desert like trunkless legs of stone, the casino managers complied with the request of Summa's public relations director for a minute of silence out of respect for Hughes. The message went out over the public-address systems and for a brief moment the casinos fell silent. Housewives stood uncomfortably clutching their paper cups of coins at the slot machines, the blackjack games paused, and at the crap tables stickmen cradled the dice in the crooks of their wooden wands.

Then a pit boss looked at his watch, leaned forward, and whispered to the stickman, "OK, roll the dice. He's had his minute."

ABOUT THE AUTHOR

JAMES PHELAN has been described by *The New York Times*' Pulitzer Prize-winner Wallace Turner as "one of the best investigative reporters of his generation." At sixty-four, Mr. Phelan's track record for the big story is a long one. Former Governor Edmund (Pat) Brown credits his re-election in 1962, when he defeated Richard Nixon, to Phelan's article in *The Reporter* magazine on the Hughes-Nixon loan. Reporting for the *Saturday Evening Post*, Phelan was the first journalist to show that former District Attorney James Garrison had no case against Clay Shaw when Garrison accused Shaw of conspiring to kill President Kennedy.

For over twenty years James Phelan has been following the career of Howard Hughes and has written about him in numerous publications, including the *Saturday Evening Post*, *Paris-Match*, *Playboy* and *The New York Times*. Mr. Phelan now lives in Long Beach, California.

THE BEST OF THE BESTSELLERS
FROM WARNER BOOKS!

FIRE AND ICE by Andrew Tobias   **(82-409, $2.25)**
The bestselling **Fire And Ice** is a fascinating inside view of Charles Revson, the cosmetics magnate who built the Revlon empire. "The perfect book; a book about a first-class s.o.b. . . . Full of facts and gossip . . . absorbing."—**Wall Street Journal. 32 pages of photographs.**

MY HEART BELONGS by Mary Martin   **(89-355, $1.95)**
"An effervescent story about a little lady who believes in the magic of make-believe and maintains a childlike enthusiasm, a sparkling joy for life she can barely contain."—**St. Louis Globe. Almost 100 photos from Mary Martin's private scrapbook.**

THE CAMERONS by Robert Crichton   **(82-497, $2.25)**
The Camerons is the story of the indomitable Maggie Drum, who washes the grime of coal-mining Pitmungo town from her beautiful face and sets out to find a man worthy of fathering her family. It is the story of the big, poor-but-proud Highlander who marries her, gives her seven children, and challenges her with an unyielding spirit of his own.

THE HAMLET WARNING by Leonard Sanders   **(89-370, $1.95)**
An international terrorist group has built an atom bomb and is using it to blackmail the United States. "A doomsday thriller."—**The New York Times**

W A Warner Communications Company

Please send me the books I have checked.

Enclose check or money order only, no cash please. Plus 35¢ per copy to cover postage and handling. N.Y. State residents add applicable sales tax.

Please allow 2 weeks for delivery.

WARNER BOOKS
P.O. Box 690
New York, N.Y. 10019

Name ....

Address ....

City .... State .... Zip ....

——— Please send me your free mail order catalog

THE BEST OF BESTSELLERS
FROM WARNER BOOKS!

FIRE ESCAPE
EXIT

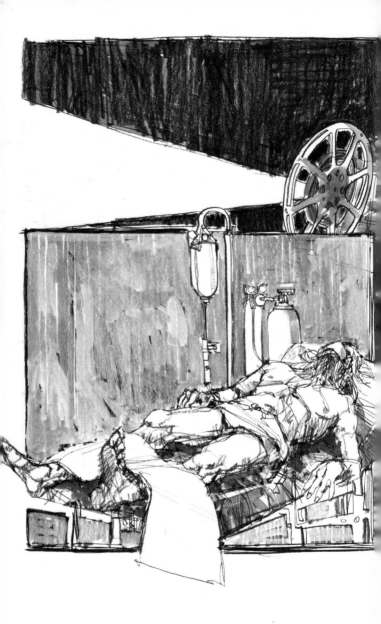